Flower Garden Plans

Created and designed by
the editorial staff of
ORTHO BOOKS

Project Editor
Joan Beth Erickson

Writer
Philip Edinger

Illustrator
Lois Lovejoy

Designer
Gary Hespenheide

Ortho Books

Publisher
Edward A. Evans

Editorial Director
Christine Jordan

Production Director
Ernie S. Tasaki

Managing Editors
Robert J. Beckstrom
Michael D. Smith
Sally W. Smith

System Manager
Linda M. Bouchard

Product Manager
Richard E. Pile, Jr.

Marketing Administrative Assistant
Daniel Stage

Distribution Specialist
Barbara F. Steadham

Operations Assistant
Georgiann Wright

Technical Consultant
J. A. Crozier, Jr., Ph.D.

Address all inquiries to:
Ortho Books
Chevron Chemical Company
Consumer Products Division
Box 5047
San Ramon, CA 94583

3	4	5	6	7	8	9
92	93	94	95	96		

ISBN 0-89721-231-2
Library of Congress Catalog Card Number 90-86163

Chevron Chemical Company
6001 Bollinger Canyon Road, San Ramon, CA 94583

Acknowledgments

Photo Editor
Sarah Bendersky

Photo Assistant
Mary Sullivan

Copy Chief
Melinda E. Levine

Editorial Coordinator
Cass Dempsey

Copyeditor
Hazel White

Proofreader
Deborah Bruner

Indexer
Shirley J. Manley

Layout and Composition by
Nancy Patton Wilson-McCune

Editorial Assistants
John Parr
Laurie A. Steele

Associate Editor
Sara Shopkow

Production by
Studio 165

Separations by
Color Tech. Corp.

Lithographed in the USA by
Webcrafters, Inc.

Special Thanks to
John C. MacGregor IV

Consultants
Frederick and Mary Ann McGourty

Photographers
Names of photographers are followed by the page numbers on which their work appears. R=right, C=center, L=left, T=top, B=bottom.

William C. Aplin/Ortho Slide Library: 20R, 55, 87B
Laurie A. Black/Ortho Slide Library: 60B
Josephine Coatsworth/Ortho Slide Library: Title page, 10CR, 10BR, 28, 34T, 41, 63, 73T, 79B, 83T, 83B, 95T, 95B, back cover TL, back cover BL
Rosalind Creasy: Front cover, 4
Karil Daniels/Ortho Slide Library: 36T
Saxon Holt/Ortho Slide Library: 12C, 24B, 73B, 80T, 87T, 90B, 100, back cover BR
Susan M. Lammers/Ortho Slide Library: 104
Michael Landis/Ortho Slide Library: 7TR, 27, 39, 44, 62, 67L, 71BL, 78, 92T, 92B
Lois Lovejoy: 73C
Michael McKinley/Ortho Slide Library: 10T, 17T, 22T, 22B, 24T, 29, 30T, 33BL, 33BR, 34B, 56, 80B, 85, 89, 97, back cover TR
James McNair/Ortho Slide Library: 10BL
Jack Napton/Ortho Slide Library: 12T, 19, 36B, 66, 67R, 71BR
Ortho Information Services: 6, 7TL, 7B, 17B, 25, 26, 30B, 47, 52, 54, 59, 71T, 74T, 74B, 75, 76T, 76B, 79T
Pam Peirce/Ortho Slide Library: 12B, 33T, 90, 100
Michael D. Smith/Ortho Slide Library: 20L
Tom Tracy/Ortho Slide Library: 24C, 38, 60T
Wolf von dem Bussche/Ortho Slide Library: 10CL, 51

Front Cover
A colorful blend of old-fashioned petunias (*Petunia violacea*), roses (*Rosa* 'Showbiz'), and garden nasturtiums (*Tropaeolum majus*) welcome you to the summer ornamental edible garden of noted author and lecturer Rosalind Creasy.

Back Cover
Top left: Lily-of-the-Nile (*Agapanthus orientalis*) make a cool-color addition to a perennials garden.

Top right: The rusty hues of stonecrop (*Sedum telephium* 'Autumn Joy') herald the arrival of a fall garden's splendor.

Bottom left: Bold and brassy gazania (*Gazania*) contribute a special brilliance to a hot and bright garden.

Bottom right: No summer garden is complete without a clematis (*Clematis × jackmanii*).

Title Page
Hollyhock (*Alcea rosea*) blooms tower above marigolds (*Tagetès*) in this flower garden border.

Flower Garden Plans

Introduction to Planning Your Flower Garden

As the pace of life accelerates and time and land assume more value. small things of beauty become increasingly precious. We can savor the grandeur of estate gardens in the sweeping landscapes of parks; but to satisfy our needs for personal expression, the greatest rewards from the least effort come from flower gardening.

V irtually everyone who has the urge to garden imagines having a garden of colorful flowers. No wonder, then, that a collection of flower garden plans will have wide appeal. A flower garden brings the promise of beauty from color—and on a manageable scale. A flower garden also can be installed without a great outlay of money or time. It could easily be a weekend do-it-yourself project.

In the following pages are 42 planting plans for gardens that address a variety of needs and interests. Should you need color at particular times of year, there are garden plans specifically for color in each of the four seasons as well as a plan for a garden that is colorful from spring into fall. A special seasonal garden is shown on the cover—a summer garden, California style, executed by author and horticulturist Rosalind Creasy, who is noted for her imaginative use of edible plants in ornamental designs. Should you want a garden that features a particular color or color group, there are plans for a white garden and a gray garden, and plans devoted to cool and warm tones, pastel shades, and color from foliage alone.

A summer garden provides a bounty of petunias and verbena and also a decorative edible, the garden nasturtium.

Another set of plans focuses on particular garden styles; these range from the studied simplicity of Japanese and desert plantings to the exuberance of the English cottage garden. Other plans reflect particular themes, such as the world of nature (hummingbird and butterfly gardens) and literature and history (Shakespeare and medieval apothecary gardens). Gardeners of a practical bent will be interested in the plans for an efficient kitchen garden and for a bed of flowers for cutting. There are plans designed for special situations: a shade planting, a low-water-use planting, and plantings for damp soil, a hillside, and a pond. And for gardeners with specific plant interests, there are individual plans for annuals, perennials, ornamental grasses, shrubs, and three different plans for roses.

the planting plan are keyed to the lists of plants for that garden. The numbers in the plan indicate the number of a particular plant that should be planted within that space. Numbers in parentheses on the plan represent the number of plants to be used from the alternative selections if this number differs from the main list plant count. (The numbers placed in parentheses after each plant in the plant lists indicate the total number of each plant needed in the entire planting scheme.) An artistic rendering shows a portion of each plan as it will look in flower, and the photographs show the main plants in detail.

PLANT CHOICE AND CARE

The plants for each plan have been selected to satisfy the widest possible gardening audience.

A Japanese garden captures the essence of tranquility. In a verdant setting sits three classic elements: a stone lantern, a pond, and a Japanese maple.

HOW TO READ THE PLANS

Each garden is presented in the same way: A planting plan illustrates the arrangement of plants within the garden. Drawn to scale, it shows the space each plant will occupy. You will also see a light grid, each square of which represents one square foot. The letters within

Each plan has at least two plant lists: a main list and an alternative list. Plants in nearly all the main lists will grow well in most gardens in USDA zone 7 (winter minimum temperatures of 0° F) and also in somewhat colder and warmer regions as well. The full USDA Hardiness Zone Map appears on page 108. The text

for each planting explains the zone tolerance. The alternative plant lists, which range from a few plants to an entirely different list, have two purposes. In many cases, they extend the usefulness of a plan into the coldest zones or into the regions that experience little or no winter chill. Where the main plant list already satisfies a broad climate range, the alternative selections list plants that will give the planting a different color slant. On some plans you will find alternative selections given for each plant, according to criteria mentioned in the text of the plan. When alternate selections aren't listed, use the plants from the main text.

Aside from zone tolerance, the other important criterion in choosing the plants for these gardens was their availability. No plants are rare, obscure, or hard to locate. Many, in fact, might be carried by well-stocked local or regional nurseries. Many also are offered by mail-order suppliers and specialty plant nurseries; for a list of reputable mail-order sources, refer to page 107.

The description of each plan includes some basic nuts-and-bolts information you'll need to ensure success. Although most of the plans have been devised to suit average garden soil and routine watering, you will find the cultural needs spelled out for each planting. And since no garden succeeds without some maintenance, the text also suggests a suitable program for routine tasks.

VARIATIONS

Each plan was designed as an individual unit, complete unto itself, but you can install any of the plantings into an existing garden provided cultural conditions are suitable. What do you do if a plan is ideal except that it is too large for your space or is not quite the right configuration? Read the material under Variations. The instructions in these sections offer at least one way to alter the size or shape of the planting while maintaining an attractive, well-designed flower garden.

Top left: Barrel and prickly pear cacti compose the classic appearance of this desert garden.
Top right: A fruit bowl mix of zinnia adds a splash of color to an annuals garden.
Bottom: A rose lends both color and fragrance to a garden, whether it's an accent plant or part of a rose bed.

Kolkwitzia

Philadelphus

Digitalis

Hemerocallis

Iris

Iberis

Myosotis

A SPRING GARDEN

The season of nature's reawakening, spring decks a garden in the year's first display of floral magnificence. Flowering shrubs, perennials, and bulbs are the mainstays of the spring garden. From modest beginnings—a scattering of aconites or crocuses, a sweep of daffodils, or a fanfare of tulips—a spring flower garden reaches a crescendo in most zones in April or May.

Though this garden reaches full flower in late spring, there is something of interest flowering throughout the season. Early spring color is provided by lily-of-the-valley, forget-me-not, candytuft, cut-leaf lilac, and the slender deutzia. Mid- to late spring color is offered by the other perennials, the beauty bush, the spiraea, and the Constance Spry rose.

The plants in the main list are appropriate for gardens in zones 7 and 8 and the colder parts of zone 9. Gardeners in zones 4, 5, and 6 should choose a Raubritter rose, from the alternative list, rather than the less cold-tolerant Constance Spry. Gardeners in Sun Belt zone 9

and arid zone 10 should plant the other recommended alternatives.

This spring garden needs a reasonably sunny spot. Locate it where it will receive at least six hours of sun each day until all the plants have finished flowering. After that, a half day of sun will suffice, though more is better. Give the plants routine garden watering.

Maintenance starts in late winter or earliest spring, when you should remove dead leaves and stems from the previous year. Deciduous shrubs flower on wood formed the previous year, so prune to remove old wood only after the flowering period. Thin out old wood on the climbing rose at the end of the dormant season, and train new growth as it matures after flowering. As the large perennials finish blooming, remove the spent flower stems or spikes. Be sure to cut off the spent blooms of Jupiter's-beard, especially in mild-winter regions: Volunteer seedlings can become a nuisance. Most of the perennials will need replacing or dividing and replanting at some time. Lily-of-the-valley and peony can remain in place indefinitely. Daylily and Siberian iris need only infrequent dividing and replanting; bearded iris needs dividing every three to four years. Foxglove, lupine, columbine, and Jupiter's-beard will need replacing as the old plants start to decline in vigor and productivity. In the warm zones (8, 9, and 10) they may last three or four years; in colder zones they may last no more than two. Basket-of-gold and candytuft also will need replacing after several years, though shearing them back after bloom will keep them compact and youthful. The forget-me-not will need replacing every two or three years, but volunteer seedlings usually ensure that there's always a new crop coming along.

Variations

In keeping with the freshness of the season, all the flower colors in this garden are clear and somewhat soft; bright, assertive tones are more the province of summer. You can vary the colors of the scheme by selecting different cultivars of peony, climbing rose, and bearded iris (some of which are decidedly assertive in color). Jupiter's-beard is available in three colors: white, dusty rose, and light crimson. Initially, the shrubs—particularly the beauty bush and cut-leaf lilac—will not fill the area indicated in the planting scheme. To achieve a fuller appearance in the early years and to cover the otherwise bare earth, enlarge the areas allotted to the neighboring perennials. Later, as the shrubs grow, you can gradually reduce the number of perennials. Alternatively, you could place several irregularly spaced clumps of foxglove around the beauty bush behind the perennials, again removing them as the beauty bush gains in size.

Spring-Garden Plants

A. *Kolkwitzia amabilis* (beauty bush) (1)
B. *Syringa laciniata* (cut-leaf lilac) (1)
C. *Philadelphus* × *virginalis* 'Glacier' (mock orange) (1)
D. *Deutzia gracilis* (slender deutzia) (1)
E. *Spiraea trilobata* 'Swan Lake' (spiraea) (1)
F. *Rosa* 'Constance Spry' (1)
G. *Paeonia lactiflora* 'Festiva Maxima' (peony) (2)
H. *Iris*, tall bearded hybrid 'Victoria Falls' (7)
I. *Iris*, Siberian hybrid 'Ego' (6)
J. *Iberis sempervirens* (evergreen candytuft) (8)
K. *Lupinus*, Russell hybrids (Russell lupines) (10)
L. *Digitalis purpurea* (common foxglove) (10)
M. *Hemerocallis* 'Stella de Oro' (daylily) (7)
N. *Convallaria majalis* (lily-of-the-valley) (18)
O. *Aquilegia*, McKana Giants strain (columbine) (10)
P. *Myosotis sylvatica* (forget-me-not) (19)
Q. *Centranthus ruber* (Jupiter's-beard) (7)
R. *Aurinia saxatilis* (basket-of-gold) (12)

Alternative Selections

A. *Raphiolepis indica* 'Enchantress' (India-hawthorn) (1)
B. *Coleonema album* (white breath-of-heaven) (1)
C. *Cistus* × 'Sunset' (rockrose) (1)
D. *Cistus skanbergii* (rockrose) (1)
E. *Ruta graveolens* (rue) (1)
F. *Rosa* 'Raubritter', for zones 4, 5, and 6 (1)
G. *Centranthus ruber* 'Albus' (white Jupiter's-beard) (2)
I. *Iris*, Spuria hybrid 'Marilyn Holloway' (6)
K. *Antirrhinum majus* (snapdragon) (10)
O. *Bergenia cordifolia* (heartleaf bergenia) (10)
Q. *Erysimum linifolium* (wallflower) (7)

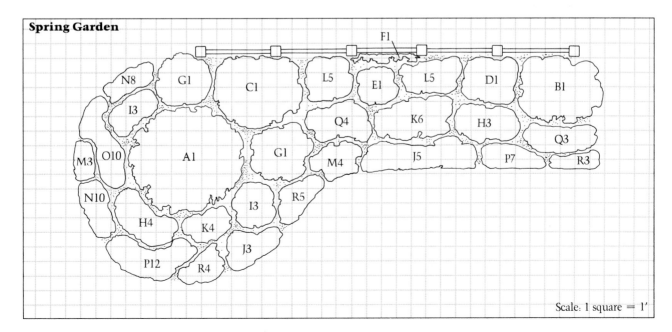

Spring Garden

Scale: 1 square = 1′

The shape of this spring garden can be changed easily. To extend the length, place more of the shrubs at intervals along the fence line, fronting and interspersing them with more of the perennials. Or plant two of each shrub, spacing the second so that it is two thirds the plant's diameter from the first; then stretch the length of each drift of perennials or add more drifts, following the patterns indicated in the plan. To shorten the bed, stop the planting at the right of the large drift of candytuft, then plant drifts of forget-me-not or basket-of-gold, or both, to the right of the lupine and foxglove. To convert the garden to a rectangle, extend the straight line of the bottom edge so that it ends at the beauty bush; eliminate all the plants below the line and to the left of the beauty bush.

Top: *Antirrhinum majus* (snapdragon)
Center left: *Digitalis purpurea* (common foxglove)
Center right: *Iberis sempervirens* (evergreen candytuft)
Bottom left: *Convallaria majalis* (lily-of-the-valley)
Bottom right: *Centranthus ruber* (Jupiter's-beard)

A SUMMER GARDEN

Summer brings the fullness of the gardening year; it's in this season that the greatest number of plants develop flowers in abundance. Summer also brings the warmest weather, signaling a time to take it easy (after you've attended to the watering) and enjoy the fruits of your gardening labors. This summer garden, therefore, features a shaded nook where you can sit, relax, and survey a riot of different flowers.

The shrubs and perennials in these summer borders will thrive in zones 5 through 9 and dry-summer zone 10. All flower over a long period, some beginning in spring, others starting in summer and continuing into fall. The roses will provide color in all three seasons. Shrubs and perennials were chosen for this plan because of their relative permanence and lower maintenance needs. They will flower year after year, except dusty-miller, which will need replacing each spring in zones 5, 6, and 7. For this garden there are two lists of alternative selections. The first lists shrubs and perennials that are especially suited to mild winters in the warmer part of zone 9 and zone 10. The second group features a set of summer annuals distributed through the framework of shrubs and

perennials. All the annuals must be planted anew every spring—an opportunity for enthusiastic gardeners to vary the planting each year with new colors and varieties.

A cool green hedge forms the backdrop in the illustration, though a wall or fence also could provide an attractive background. The main plant list and the first list of alternatives include hedging shrubs that you should consider optional. If you choose to plant a hedge, remember to allow space for it to broaden beyond the confines of the bed.

Although the hedge, fence, or wall on three sides will shade this garden a little each day, this is a full sun planting. Each part should have at least six hours of daily sun during the growing season. The plants need routine garden watering.

In late winter or early spring, prune and thin the vines and shrubs (except for the smoke tree) to keep them shapely and productive. Clean out the dead stems and leaves of the perennials and remove the spent annuals. Divide and replant any perennials that are overcrowded and declining in performance. During the summer bloom season, cut back the spent flowering spikes of delphinium and beardtongue; this will encourage a second flowering.

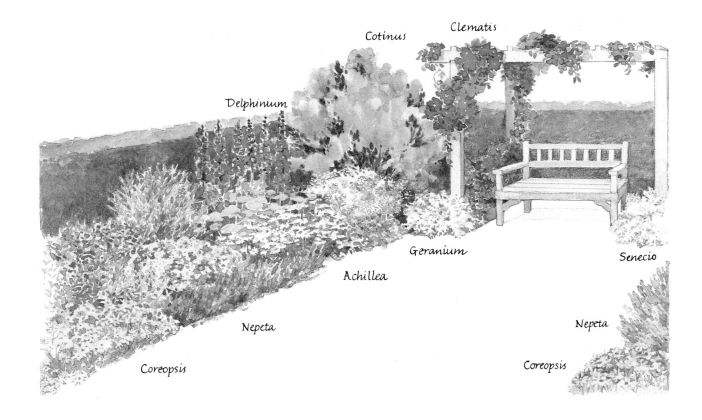

Chrysanthemum frutescens (marguerite)

Clematis × jackmanii (Jackman clematis)

Agapanthus orientalis (lily-of-the-Nile)

Summer-Garden Plants

A. *Cotinus coggygria* 'Royal Purple' (smoke tree) (1)
B. *Hibiscus syriacus* 'Diana' (rose-of-Sharon) (1)
C. *Clematis × jackmanii* (Jackman clematis) (1)
D. *Taxus × media* 'Hicksii' or *Tsuga canadensis* (Canada hemlock) planted 4 feet apart
E. *Rosa* 'Pink Meidilland' (2)
F. *Rosa* 'Ballerina' (1)
G. *Potentilla ×* 'Katherine Dykes' (shrubby cinquefoil) (2)
H. *Caryopteris × clandonensis* (blue-mist) (5)
I. *Delphinium*, Pacific hybrids (15)
J. *Achillea filipendulina* 'Coronation Gold' (fernleaf yarrow) (11)
K. *Chrysanthemum × superbum* 'Alaska' (Shasta daisy) (5)
L. *Chrysanthemum × superbum* 'Snow Lady' (Shasta daisy) (6)
M. *Perovskia atriplicifolia* (Russian sage) (4)
N. *Gypsophila paniculata* 'Viette's Dwarf' (baby's-breath) (6)
O. *Penstemon barbatus* (beardtongue) (20)
P. *Coreopsis verticillata* 'Moonbeam' (coreopsis) (8)
Q. *Hemerocallis* 'Winning Ways' (daylily) (8)
R. *Spiraea × bumalda* 'Anthony Waterer' (spiraea) (4)
S. *Nepeta × faassenii* (catmint) (10)
T. *Geranium endressii* 'Wargrave Pink' (cranesbill) (3)
U. *Stachys byzantina* 'Silver Carpet' (lamb's-ears) (9)
V. *Senecio cineraria* (dusty-miller) (8)

Alternative Selections I

B. *Nerium oleander* 'Casablanca' (oleander) (1)
C. *Jasminum grandiflorum* (Spanish jasmine) (1)
D. *Ilex vomitoria* (yaupon) or *Podocarpus macrophyllus* (yew-pine) planted 4 feet apart
G. *Agapanthus orientalis* (lily-of-the-Nile) (2)
H. *Chrysanthemum frutescens* (marguerite) (5)
I. *Malva alcea* var. *fastigiata* (mallow) (15)
R. *Salvia leucantha* (Mexican bush sage) (4)

Alternative Selections II

L. *Catharanthus roseus* (Madagascar periwinkle) (6)
R. *Nicotiana alata* 'Sensation' (flowering tobacco) (4)
S. *Verbena × hybrida* (garden verbena) (10)
T. *Celosia cristata* 'Plumosa', pink or gold selection (plume cockscomb) (3)

Summer Garden

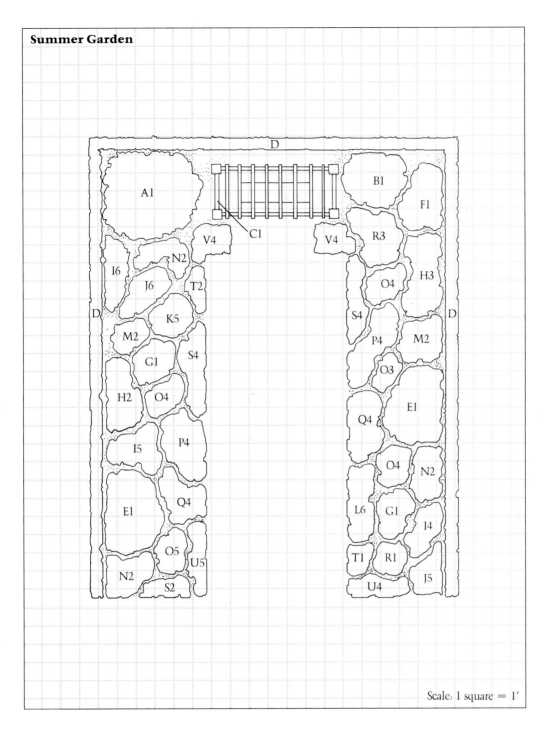

Scale: 1 square = 1'

Variations

The predominant colors in this summer garden are pink, yellow, white, and blue—bright but not strident. For hot colors, such as orange, red, and bronze, choose different cultivars of the shrub roses, rose-of-Sharon, shrubby cinquefoil, daylily, and coreopsis. Or select bright-colored annuals from the second list of alternatives.

If a double border is too elaborate for your space, you can plant either border as a rectangular bed facing a lawn or pathway. Simply continue the front line to the back wall, past either the smoke tree (on left) or rose-of-Sharon (right); finish off the front of the border with narrow drifts of coreopsis, catmint, or both. To make one long border, rotate the right-hand border so that it extends the left one, abutting the two Pink Meidilland roses and eliminating the plants that overlap in the superimposition. This will give you a bed 40 to 45 feet long, with the smoke tree at one end of the planting and the rose-of-Sharon and Ballerina rose at the other.

A SUMMER ORNAMENTAL, EDIBLE GARDEN

A stroll up two steps and down the path leads you to the front door of author and lecturer Rosalind Creasy, noted proponent of ornamental edible gardens. Although plants grown strictly for flowers predominate in this summer entryway garden (pictured on the cover of this book), a close look reveals several edibles tucked into the planting scheme: sweet peppers, rhubarb chard, and oriental bunching onions for cooking or salads; chives; two kinds of thyme; chamomile for tea; and nasturtiums for garnishes and salads.

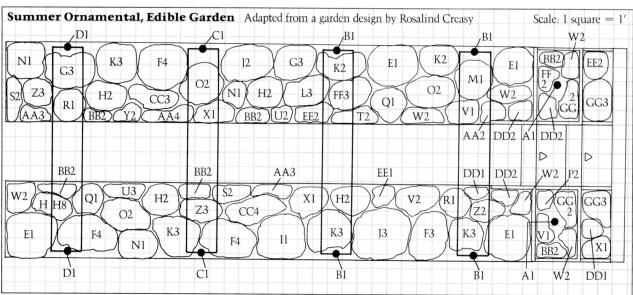

Summer Ornamental, Edible Garden   Adapted from a garden design by Rosalind Creasy   Scale: 1 square = 1'

Summer Ornamental, Edible Plants

A. *Rosa* 'Showbiz', as a 36-inch standard (2)
B. *Ipomoea acuminata* (blue dawnflower) (4)
C. *Humulus lupulus* (common hop) (2)
D. *Vigna caracalla* (snail vine) (2)
E. *Lavandula angustifolia* (English lavender) (4)
F. *Chrysanthemum × superbum* (Shasta daisy) (15)
G. *Chrysanthemum × morifolium* (florists chrysanthemum) (6)
H. *Sedum telephium* 'Autumn Joy' (stonecrop) (8)
I. *Dahlia*, informal decorative hybrid (1)
J. *Origanum laevigatum* 'Hopley's' (oregano) (5)
K. *Penstemon × gloxinioides* (border penstemon) (16)
L. *Penstemon barbatus* (beardtongue) (3)
M. *Punica granatum* 'Nana' (dwarf pomegranate) (1)
N. *Physostegia virginiana* 'Summer Snow' (false-dragonhead) (3)
O. *Calceolaria integrifolia* 'Golden Nugget' (slipper flower) (6)
P. *Echeveria × imbricata* (hen-and-chicks) (2)
Q. *Thymus × citriodorus* (lemon thyme) (2)
R. *Thymus vulgaris* 'Argenteus' (silver thyme) (2)
S. *Diascia* 'Ruby Field' (twinspur) (4)
T. *Chamaemelum nobile* (chamomile) (2)
U. *Allium schoenoprasum* (chives) (5)
V. *Geranium* 'Johnson's Blue' (cranesbill) (4)
W. *Verbena tenuisecta* (moss verbena) (12)
X. *Nepeta × faassenii* (catmint) (3)
Y. *Viola × wittrockiana* (pansy) (2)
Z. *Beta vulgaris cicla* 'Rhubarb' (rhubarb chard) (8)
AA. *Lobelia erinus* 'Crystal Palace' (lobelia) (12)
BB. *Lobularia maritima* (sweet alyssum) (12)
CC. *Capsicum annuum* (sweet pepper) (7)
DD. *Tropaeolum majus* (garden nasturtium, dwarf) (8)
EE. *Tagetes tenuifolia* 'Lemon Gem' (signet marigold) (4)
FF. *Dahlia*, bedding type (5)
GG. *Petunia violacea* (old-fashioned petunia) (10)
HH. *Allium fistulosum* (oriental bunching onion) (8)

Alternative Selections

B. *Ipomoea tricolor* (morning glory) (4)
D. *Phaseolus coccineus* (scarlet runner bean) (2)
E. *Caryopteris × clandonensis* (blue-mist) (4)
K. *Lythrum virgatum* 'Dropmore Purple' (purple loosestrife) (16)
M. *Potentilla* 'Gold Drop' (cinquefoil) (1)
O. *Achillea ×* 'Moonshine' (yarrow) (6)
P. *Sempervivum tectorum* (hen-and-chickens) (2)
S. *Heuchera sanguinea* (coralbells) (4)
W. *Campanula portenschlagiana* (*C. muralis*) (Dalmatian bellflower) (12)

From mid-spring through summer this double border presents a colorful welcome. In this dry-summer zone 9 garden, the vanguards of the display are pansies, nasturtiums, and chives, closely followed by lobelia and sweet alyssum. By early summer nearly all the plants are showing color or are in full flower. Overhead, the lightweight arbor that ties the two borders together is entwined with blue dawnflower, snail vine, and hops. Good soil, regular watering by drip irrigation, and full sun make this garden the success that it is in dry-summer zone 9. You can expect similar success in dry-summer zones 8 and 10; for zones 6 and 7 and moist-summer zones 8 and 9, choose plants from the alternative selections.

Maintenance begins in late fall with a little clean up. Remove spent stems of the perennials and played-out annuals and vegetables. In late winter, just before the growing season, clear out the dead foliage and stems of the vines, stonecrop, cranesbill, and dahlias. Cut back to the ground the stems of florists chrysanthemum, Shasta daisy, false-dragonhead, and oregano. Reduce both the border penstemon and beardtongue to a few inches, and cut back nearly all growth on the catmint. Cut back the English lavender and Showbiz rose by about half. In late winter or early spring start thinking about the annuals. Set out the pansy plants while the weather is cool; and plant nasturtium seeds and plants of lobelia, sweet alyssum, Lemon Gem marigold, and sweet peppers when the soil has warmed.

After several years, you'll need either to replace the perennials or to dig them up and divide them. When these plants start to decline, replace them: rhubarb chard, border penstemon, beardtongue, slipper flower, lemon and silver thyme, and twinspur. When these plants start to decline, dig them up and divide them: Shasta daisy, florists chrysanthemum, dahlia, stonecrop, false-dragonhead, hen-and-chicks, and catmint.

Variations

In this garden, the visitor ascends steps between raised beds to reach the level path bounded by the long, narrow borders. For a level or gently sloping site, you can eliminate the raised beds that contain the standard roses; this will give you a shorter double border.

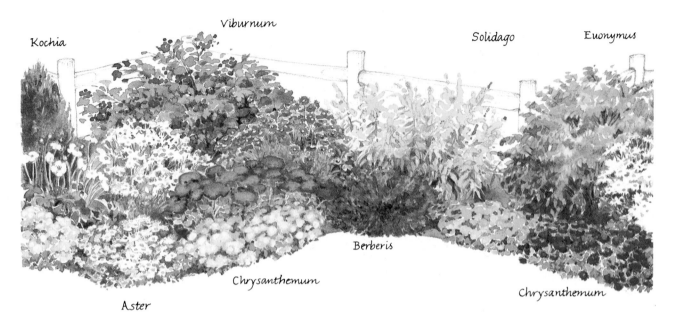

Kochia Viburnum Solidago Euonymus

Berberis

Chrysanthemum Chrysanthemum

Aster

A FALL GARDEN

In regions where winter is distinct, fall heralds
the close of the growing season. The last crops
are ready for harvest, foliage changes to brilliant colors, and berries that will provide winter
food for wildlife start to ripen. Yet fall also provides a final burst of flowers as an encore to
summer's heady displays. As sure as the season
gives us football, it also brings on chrysanthemums, and the other daisy relatives, including a
selected form of that sometimes-weed goldenrod.

This fall planting mingles all the colorful
elements of the season. Vibrant red autumn
foliage accompanies flowers in comple-
mentary yellow and bronze tones plus contrasting blue shades and white; the European
cranberry bush provides bright red fruits.
Flowering will begin in late summer and continue into November or until frost calls a halt.
The plants in the main list are for gardens in
zones 4 through 9. For gardens in zones 3 and
10, use the appropriate alternative selection.
Plants in all three lists need full sun and normal garden watering.

In mild-winter zones, you can get a
headstart on maintenance by removing spent
flower stems during the winter. With the
perennials trimmed back, the garden will have
a far neater appearance. In colder regions—
especially where snow blurs the outlines of the

plantings—begin maintenance in late winter
or early spring. After you've tidied up dead
leaves and anemone stems and removed the
dead plants of the annual Mexican fire bush,
cut back the chrysanthemum, asters, boltonia,
and goldenrod. If the perennials are losing
vigor, divide and reset them just after the new
growth begins. Spring is also the time to replace plants. Once the soil starts to warm, set
out new plants of the annual Mexican fire
bush and perhaps also of the cushion-type
chrysanthemums, which may be short-lived in
zones 4, 5, and 6.

Variations

The simplest variations to this garden come
from changing the color scheme. You can
choose among a wide range of chrysanthemum
colors and pink anemones in addition to white
ones and asters that are white, blue-purple, or
pink-red instead of just blue. Be careful,
though, about placing some cold pink shades
next to the reds of the autumn leaves.

For a change in shape, consider a nearly
round garden. Eliminating the left-hand segment (which contains the Mexican fire bush)
leaves a nearly complete semicircle. Sketch
this part of the plan and you'll find that its
mirror image, turned upside down, interlocks
with the main plan to form a near-circular bed.

Fall-Garden Plants

A. *Viburnum opulus* 'Compactum' (European cranberry bush) (2)
B. *Euonymus alata* 'Compacta' (winged euonymus) (2)
C. *Solidago* 'Golden Mosa' (goldenrod) (10)
D. *Spiraea* × *bumalda* 'Goldflame' (spiraea) (3)
E. *Aster novi-belgii*, dwarf blue selection, such as 'Audrey' or 'Royal Opal' (New York aster) (8)
F. *Anemone* × *hybrida* 'Honorine Jobert' (Japanese anemone) (6)
G. *Aster novi-belgii*, tall dark blue selection, such as 'Eventide' (New York aster) (2)
H. *Boltonia asteroides* 'Snowbank' (boltonia) (6)
I. *Berberis thunbergii* 'Crimson Pygmy' (Japanese barberry) (1)
J. *Sedum telephium* 'Autumn Joy' (stonecrop) (3)
K. *Chrysanthemum*, cushion-mum type in bronze, yellow, cream colors (26)
L. *Kochia scoparia trichophylla* (Mexican fire bush) (7)

Alternative Selections, Zone 3

A. *Viburnum trilobum* 'Compactum' (cranberry bush) (2)
B. *Cornus alba* 'Sibirica' (Siberian dogwood) (2)
D. *Aster novi-belgii*, dwarf white selection, such as 'Snowball' or 'Snow Flurry' (New York aster) (5)
I. *Aster novi-belgii*, dwarf blue selection, such as 'Audrey' or 'Royal Opal' (New York aster) (4)

Alternative Selections, Zone 10

B. *Miscanthus sinensis* 'Purpurascens' (eulalia-grass) (3)
D. *Anthemis tinctoria* 'Moonlight' (golden marguerite) (6)
I. *Imperata cylindrica* 'Rubra' (Japanese bloodgrass) (3)

Sedum telephium 'Autumn Joy' (stonecrop)

Berberis thunbergii (Japanese barberry)

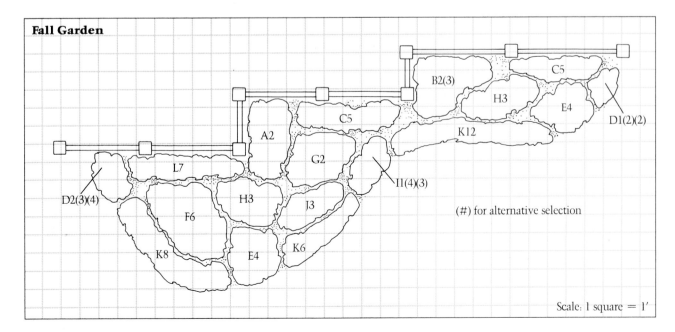

Fall Garden

B2(3) C5 H3 E4 D1(2)(2) C5 K12 A2 G2 I1(4)(3) L7 D2(3)(4) H3 F6 J3 K8 E4 K6

(#) for alternative selection

Scale: 1 square = 1′

A WINTER GARDEN

Despite the phrase "dead of winter," the season can offer color—even flower color. The catch is, it depends on where you live. In northern and mountain regions, where winter means a steady blanket of snow, garden color in winter is a sometime thing, chiefly derived from evergreens, berried deciduous shrubs (before birds strip them), and the bright bark of certain dogwoods and willows. By contrast, gardeners in zone 10 and the warmer parts of zone 9 can plan for colorful flowers that will reliably enliven this least active but far-from-dead season. Between these two extremes lie the regions where snow may or may not occur, comes and goes, or arrives late and leaves early. This patchy snow most often occurs in zones 6 through 8, though some zone 5 gardeners will find it familiar.

The planting scheme for this winter garden was designed for these zones, 6 through 8, especially the northeast, eastern seaboard, upper South, and Pacific Northwest. Winter-blooming heaths and Christmas-rose carry the banner of flower color in white and pink. The dogwood and Japanese maple present red stems and bark; the European cranberry bush offers striking clusters of red berries on leafless branches. The paxistima, juniper, and arborvitae contribute foliage that is, respectively, bronze, purplish, and golden.

The alternative plant selections are appropriate for zone 9, and also for most gardens in zone 8. The warmer climate allows an expanded range of flowering plants: a Lenten-rose, viola, primrose, bergenia, laurustinus, and camellia. The alternative scheme retains the Japanese maple for its coral red stems and bark which are a standout. Foliage color derives from the dwarf heavenly-bamboo and the dwarf golden arborvitae.

The main planting needs sun for at least six hours each day. To satisfy the heaths, the soil must be well drained and moisture retentive. The alternative planting needs partial shade or filtered sunlight for about half the day to accommodate the camellias and Lenten-rose.

Minimum maintenance is a bonus with this planting. In fall, after the leaves have dropped, rake off the ones that cover the low plants. In spring, clean out any unsightly dead foliage on the perennials. After the heaths have stopped flowering, shear off the spent stems to keep the plants dense and compact. In the alternative planting, you will need to replace the violas each year in fall.

Cornus

Acer

Helleborus

Erica 'Winter Beauty'

Erica 'Springwood'

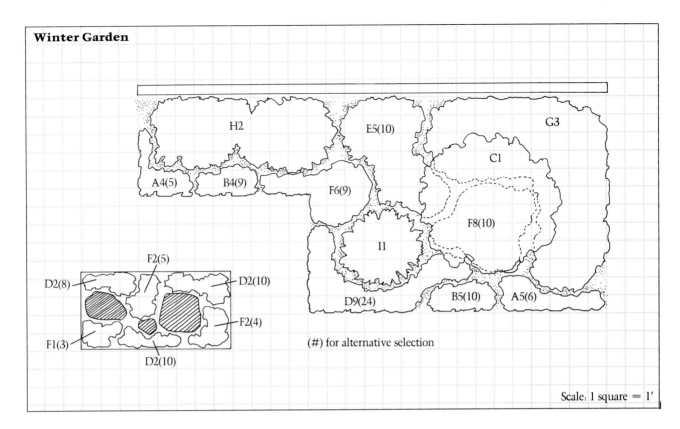

Winter Garden

H2

E5(10)

G3

C1

A4(5)   B4(9)

F6(9)

F8(10)

I1

F2(5)

D2(8)

D2(10)

F2(4)

F1(3)

D2(10)

D9(24)   B5(10)   A5(6)

(#) for alternative selection

Scale: 1 square = 1′

Although the primroses are perennials, in the warmest areas you will get the best display by setting out new plants each fall.

Variations

This garden is deliberately small—a fragment of color to cherish during the winter. The square island bed is optional. As shown, it features a moorland patch of heaths and rock. However, it could just as easily contain a bench nestled among heaths (or Lenten-rose and primroses), a place to contemplate these special wintertime offerings.

Helleborus niger (Christmas-rose)

Winter-Garden Plants
A. *Paxistima canbyi* (cliff-green) (9)
B. *Helleborus niger* (Christmas-rose) (9)
C. *Acer palmatum* 'Sangokaku' (Japanese maple) (1)
D. *Erica carnea* 'Springwood' (heath) (9, or 15 with optional bed)
E. *Juniperus horizontalis* 'Plumosa' (Andorra juniper) (5)
F. *Erica carnea* 'Winter Beauty' (heath) (14, or 19 with optional bed)
G. *Viburnum opulus* 'Compactum' (European cranberry bush) (3)
H. *Cornus alba* 'Sibirica' (Siberian dogwood) (2)
I. *Thuja occidentalis* 'Rheingold' (American arborvitae) (1)

Alternative Selections
A. *Helleborus orientalis* (Lenten-rose) (11)
B. *Viola cornuta* (viola) (19)
D. *Primula* × *polyantha* (polyanthus primrose) (24, or 52 with optional bed)
E. *Nandina domestica* 'Harbour Dwarf' (heavenly-bamboo) (10)
F. *Bergenia crassifolia* (winter-blooming bergenia) (19, or 31 with optional bed)
G. *Viburnum tinus* 'Spring Bouquet' (laurustinus) (3)
H. *Camellia japonica* 'C.M. Wilson' or 'Shiro Chan' (2)
I. *Platycladus orientalis* 'Aureus' (dwarf golden arborvitae) (1)

A THREE-SEASON GARDEN

If you want a garden that will offer attractions throughout the growing season, consider this three-season scheme that provides color from spring into fall. Although the color may not at all times match the intense color found in the spring garden or the summer gardens, this planting definitely doesn't fall short in either beauty or interest. Here, you will be especially aware of the attractiveness of the individual plants and the pleasing associations of foliage and flowers.

All plants in this scheme were chosen for their long period of bloom (the roses, in fact, flower in all three seasons). Rather than bursts and gaps, there will be a flowering continuum. The backbone of the garden is formed by shrubs—chosen for their foliage as much as for their flowers. Perennials make up the remainder of the scheme, though the alternative selections list suggests three long-blooming annuals that you could substitute for some of the foreground drifts. Plants in the main list will thrive in zones 5 through 9, although in zones 5 and 6 the floribunda roses will need winter protection and the beardtongue may need replacing every two or three years. With the first six substitutions in the alternatives list, the planting also will succeed in the dry-summer regions of zone 10. In all zones, locate the planting in full sun and give it routine garden watering.

Late winter and early spring are the times to perform basic maintenance. Prune roses, rose-of-Sharon, and blue-mist to shape and re-move any unproductive wood. Cut back the

Three-Season Garden Plants

A. *Cotinus coggygria* 'Royal Purple' (smoke tree) (1)
B. *Hibiscus syriacus* 'Diana' (rose-of-Sharon) (1)
C. *Rosa* 'Bonica' (2)
D. *Rosa* 'Iceberg' (2)
E. *Rosa* 'Class Act' (5)
F. *Weigela florida* 'Variegata' (variegated weigela) (4)
G. *Caryopteris* × *clandonensis* (blue-mist) (4)
H. *Berberis thunbergii* 'Atropurpurea' (redleaf Japanese barberry) (2)
I. *Perovskia atriplicifolia* (Russian sage) (6)
J. *Boltonia asteroides* 'Snowbank' (boltonia) (2)
K. *Aster novi-belgii,* tall blue cultivar (New York aster) (6)
L. *Achillea decolorans* 'W.B. Child' (yarrow) (6)
M. *Achillea filipendulina* 'Coronation Gold' (fernleaf yarrow) (5)
N. *Heliopsis helianthoides scabra* (false-sunflower) (7)
O. *Coreopsis verticillata* 'Moonbeam' (coreopsis) (6)
P. *Sedum telephium* 'Autumn Joy' (stonecrop) (5)
Q. *Hemerocallis* 'Evergold' (daylily) (4)
R. *Hemerocallis* 'Stella de Oro' (daylily) (3)
S. *Penstemon barbatus* 'Prairie Fire' (beardtongue) (14)
T. *Stachys byzantina* (lamb's-ears) (9)
U. *Bergenia crassifolia* (winter-blooming bergenia) (8)
V. *Nepeta* × *faassenii* (catmint) (9)

Alternative Selections

B. *Nerium oleander* 'Casablanca', for zone 10 (oleander) (1)
F. *Teucrium fruticans,* for zone 10 (bush germander) (4)
G. *Chrysanthemum frutescens,* for zone 10 (marguerite) (4)
H. *Dietes bicolor,* for zone 10 (fortnight-lily) (2)
I. *Centranthus ruber* 'Albus', for zone 10 (white Jupiter's-beard) (6)
N. *Echinacea purpurea,* for zone 10 (purple coneflower) (7)
P. *Tagetes patula* (French marigold) (16)
T. *Petunia* × *hybrida* (petunia) (9)
V. *Catharanthus roseus* (Madagascar periwinkle) (9)

Left: *Tagetes* (marigold)
Right: *Rosa* 'Iceberg'

Hibiscus

Weigela

Rosa

Nepeta

Coreopsis

Bergenia

Three-Season Garden

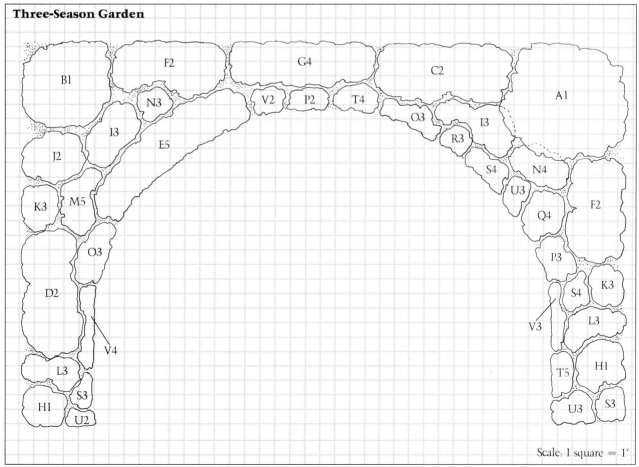

Scale: 1 square = 1'

Petunia × hybrida
(petunia)

perennials that send up flowering stems from clumps or woody bases, and remove any dead leaves from last year's growth. After the weigela flowers, prune or thin as needed. Remove the spent rose blossom clusters when they become untidy.

Variations

The crescent design with a promenade path provides a pleasant stroll as well as a possible focal point at the end of a garden. Cut the scheme in half (slicing through the blue-mist) and either the left or right side becomes a corner bed. Either half will fulfill the promise of color in three seasons.

Stachys byzantina
(lamb's-ears)

Clethra

Hibiscus

Perovskia

Lonicera

Anthemis

A WHITE GARDEN

A garden of white flowers has an undeniably romantic appeal. On a sunny day it is refreshing; in cloudy or foggy weather it is soft and luminous. And at night it becomes shadowy, ethereal, otherworldly: a setting out of *A Midsummer Night's Dream.*

Many so-called white gardens admit flowers of pale cream, ice blue, and blush pink in addition to pure white. Except for the blue-flowered Russian sage, this planting scheme favors truly white blossoms, augmented by plants that have gray or silvery white foliage (some of which have insignificant flowers of yellow or blue). If you want a white-flowered substitute for the Russian sage, choose colewort from the alternative selections; colewort produces a 6-foot-tall cloud of tiny white flowers. Although the greatest variety of flowers will appear in summer, the plants bloom from spring into fall. When there are fewer flowers, the gray and silver foliage emphasizes the overall whiteness. The main planting succeeds in zones 7 and 8 and the colder parts of zone 9. For gardens in zones 5 and 6, plant the suggested alternative climbing rose and substitute lamb's-ears for the lavender-cotton. For zone 9 or 10 gardens, substitute the other selections.

Place this white garden where it will receive six or more hours of sunlight a day during the growing season, and see that plants receive normal garden watering.

Because the planting includes shrubs, perennials, and annuals, maintenance is varied. The honeysuckle hedge shouldn't need regular trimming—it grows compact and hedgelike without shearing—but occasionally you may need to head back wayward growth. Each year in late winter, assess the other shrubs (roses, summersweet, European cranberry bush) and do whatever pruning is necessary to keep them shapely. Late winter or early spring also is the time to tidy up the perennials, dividing and replanting, or replacing, any that have declined in vigor. Cut down last year's spent stems of those that die back to ground level each fall or winter. Head back by up to half the shrubby kinds, like the Powis Castle artemisia and lavender-cotton to keep the plants compact and leafy. When the soil has warmed, set out plants of the one annual—deliciously fragrant flowering tobacco. To ensure that the evergreen candytuft survive the winter in zones 5 and 6, lightly cover the plants with cut evergreen boughs in late fall before snow covers the garden.

Variations

If the double-armed planting occupies more space than you have available, you can make a rectangular bed 24 feet long by 8 feet wide. Take the front edge of either arm and extend it across the paved area to the wall or fence and plant only that rectangle. This reduces the paved seating area to a triangle, but it will still have room enough for a chair or small bench.

Iberis sempervirens (evergreen candytuft)

Agapanthus orientalis 'Albidus' (white lily-of-the-Nile)

Anemone × hybrida 'Honorine Jobert' (Japanese anemone)

White-Garden Plants

A. *Clethra alnifolia* (summersweet) (1)
B. *Rosa* 'Blanc Double de Coubert' (3)
C. *Dictamnus albus* (gasplant) (3)
D. *Rosa* 'White Dawn' (1)
E. *Viburnum opulus* 'Compactum' (European cranberry bush) (3)
F. *Boltonia asteroides* 'Snowbank' (boltonia) (6)
G. *Hibiscus syriacus* 'Diana' (rose-of-Sharon) (1)
H. *Lonicera × xylosteoides* 'Clavey's Dwarf' (honeysuckle) (12)
I. *Artemisia ×* 'Powis Castle' (3)
J. *Gypsophila paniculata* 'Bristol Fairy' (baby's-breath) (4)
K. *Perovskia atriplicifolia* (Russian sage) (5)
L. *Paeonia lactiflora*, white cultivar (peony) (3)
M. *Anemone × hybrida* 'Honorine Jobert' (Japanese anemone) (6)
N. *Delphinium ×* 'Galahad' (delphinium) (7)
O. *Chrysanthemum × superbum* 'Snow Lady' (Shasta daisy) (12)
P. *Sedum spectabile* 'Star Dust' (stonecrop) (1)
Q. *Iris*, Siberian hybrid 'Little White' (1)
R. *Iris*, Siberian hybrid 'White Swirl' (4)
S. *Santolina chamaecyparissus* (lavender-cotton) (4)
T. *Iberis sempervirens* (evergreen candytuft) (10)
U. *Nicotiana alata* 'Grandiflora' (flowering tobacco) (18)
V. *Anthemis cupaniana*, in pot (anthemis) (1)
W. *Rosa* 'Iceberg' as a standard, in container; alternative for statuary (1)

Alternative Selections

A. *Nerium oleander* 'Casablanca' (oleander) (1)
C. *Chrysanthemum frutescens* 'Snow White' (marguerite) (3)
D. *Rosa* 'Mme. Plantier', for zones 5 and 6 (1)
E. *Teucrium fruticans* (bush germander) (3)
G. *Cistus ladanifer* (crimson-spot rockrose) (1)
H. *Myrtus communis* 'Compacta Variegata' (variegated dwarf myrtle) (12)
J. *Achillea ptarmica* 'The Pearl' (yarrow) (6)
K. *Crambe cordifolia* (colewort) (2)
L. *Centranthus ruber* 'Albus' (white Jupiter's-beard) (3)
Q. *Agapanthus ×* 'Rancho White' or × 'Peter Pan White' (lily-of-the-Nile) (1)
R. *Agapanthus orientalis* 'Albidus' (white lily-of-the-Nile) (4)
S. *Stachys byzantina* 'Silver Carpet' (lamb's-ears) (9)

Paeonia lactiflora
(peony)

White Garden

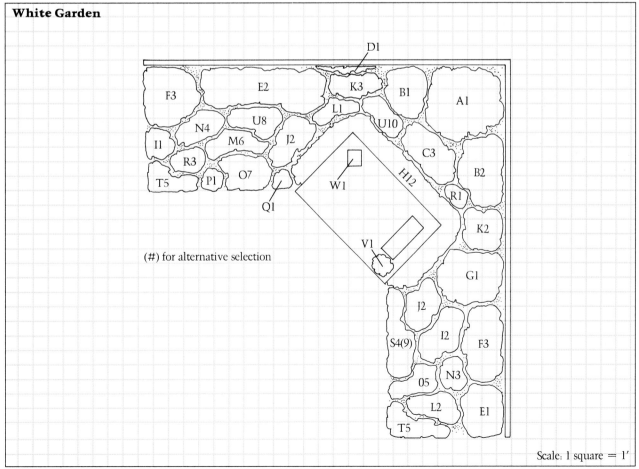

D1

F3   E2   K3   B1   A1

L1   U10

N4   U8   C3   B2

I1   J2   U10

M6

R3   O7   H12   R1

T5   P1   W1   K2

Q1

V1   G1

(#) for alternative selection

J2

S4(9)   I2   F3

O5   N3

L2   E1

T5

Scale: 1 square = 1′

Magnolia

Caryopteris

Chrysanthemum

Perovskia

Campanula

Nepeta

Stachys byzantina (lamb's-ears)

A COOL-TONES GARDEN

A garden of cool tones contains the essential elements of a white garden (see pages 23 to 25), but alters the mood by including flowers in shades of blue and violet. Although a purely white garden is cool and light, even bright in full sunlight, the addition of blue provides a shadowy element that registers "cool" even on the hottest days. A special moment occurs at twilight when the blues glow as though from light of their own.

This planting scheme provides an impressive floral display from late spring through late summer—the time of year you would want to sit on the terrace and soak up the coolness. And there will be some flowers over an even longer period: magnolia in early spring and aster, sage, and roses in fall. The main planting serves gardens in zones 5 through 9; the alternative selections extend the scheme into the dry-summer part of zone 10, although these plants will thrive in zone 9 as well.

All but one of the plants appreciate full sun: a minimum of six hours per day. The exception—the bigleaf hydrangea—prefers a half day of sun where summers are hot, or dappled or filtered sunlight throughout the day. As it gains height, the magnolia will shade the bigleaf hydrangea.

Lavandula angustifolia (English lavender)

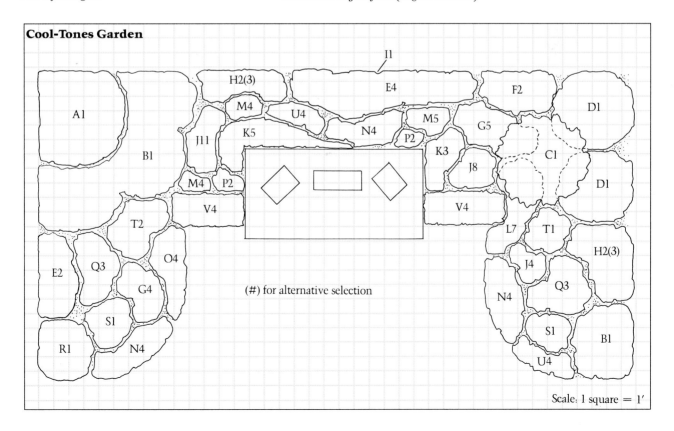

Cool-Tones Garden

I1

H2(3)

E4

F2

A1

M4

U4

M5

D1

K5

N4

G5

J11

P2

K3

C1

B1

J8

D1

M4   P2

V4

V4

T2

L7   T1

H2(3)

O4

J4

E2   Q3

Q3

G4

N4

(#) for alternative selection

S1

S1

R1   N4

B1

U4

Scale: 1 square = 1′

Cool-Tones Garden Plants

A. *Buddleia davidii* 'Empire Blue' or other blue cultivar (common butterfly bush) (1)
B. *Rosa* 'Blanc Double de Coubert' (4)
C. *Magnolia* × *loebneri* 'Merrill' (1)
D. *Hydrangea macrophylla* 'Tricolor' (bigleaf hydrangea) (2)
E. *Caryopteris* × *clandonensis* (blue-mist) (6)
F. *Lavandula angustifolia* (English lavender) (2)
G. *Aster* × *frikartii* (aster) (9)
H. *Crambe cordifolia* (colewort) (4)
I. *Clematis lanuginosa* 'Candida' (1)
J. *Salvia* × *superba* (sage) (23)
K. *Cerastium tomentosum* (snow-in-summer) (8)
L. *Campanula portenschlagiana* (Dalmatian bellflower) (7)
M. *Chrysanthemum* × *superbum* (Shasta daisy) (13)
N. *Nepeta* × *faassenii* (catmint) (12)
O. *Santolina chamaecyparissus* (lavender-cotton) (4)
P. *Iris*, Siberian hybrid 'White Swirl' (4)
Q. *Centranthus ruber* 'Albus' (white Jupiter's-beard) (6)
R. *Potentilla* × 'Abbotswood' (cinquefoil) (1)
S. *Ruta graveolens* 'Jackman's Blue' (rue) (2)
T. *Baptisia australis* (false-indigo) (3)
U. *Stachys byzantina* (lamb's-ears) (8)
V. *Perovskia atriplicifolia* (Russian sage) (8)

Alternative Selections

E. *Teucrium fruticans* (bush germander) (6)
H. *Salvia leucantha* (Mexican bush sage) (6)
I. *Solanum jasminoides* (potato vine) (1)
R. *Artemisia* × 'Powis Castle' (artemisia) (1)
V. *Lavandula angustifolia* 'Hidcote' or 'Munstead' (English lavender) (8)

Late winter or early spring, weather permitting, is the time for major maintenance. Most shrubs (except the magnolia, cinquefoil, and bush germander) will need some amount of regular pruning: the roses merely trimmed to shape, the English lavender and hydrangea cut back to about half, the common butterfly bush and blue-mist cut back to about 12 inches. Tidy up the perennials, removing dead leaves and last year's spent stems. Cut back the lavender-cotton and artemisia by one half to two thirds to keep them compact. Cut back the catmint, Russian sage, and Mexican bush sage nearly to the ground. In time, most of the perennials will need dividing and replanting.

Variations

The size and shape of this planting can be changed in several ways. To create a rectangle of the full width, draw a line from one side of the plan to the other at the lower edge of the hedge of Russian sage (or English lavender if you are using the alternative selections). Eliminate all plants below this line and extend the Russian sage (or English lavender) to the roses on the left side of the plan and to the hydrangeas on the right. For a narrower (and less symmetrical) scheme, extend either vertical edge to the top of the plan, cutting off the ends of the hedge of Russian sage (or English lavender). This leaves you with an L-shaped plan, the short arm containing either the side with common butterfly bush and three roses or hydrangeas and magnolia.

Chrysanthemum ×
superbum
(Shasta daisy)

A PASTEL-SHADES GARDEN

Colors and color associations not only affect the mood of a planting, they also alter our perceptions of space. This garden composed of pastel tones and tints suggests springtime, freshness. It also seems more distant and smaller than it would if it were planted with vibrant reds, yellows, and other equally attention-compelling colors. Set this planting into a sizable lawn and the eye will be encouraged to look past it as well as at it. In a small garden the soft pastel colors will give a sense of depth, whereas bright colors would seem to foreshorten and shrink the space.

The assortment of shrubs and perennials in this garden will show color from mid-spring to early autumn, reaching a peak in early to mid-summer. The several gray-foliaged plants both contribute to the overall pastel tones and provide color throughout the growing season. All plants on the main list except peony will prosper in zones 5 through 9 if the site receives full sun. In zone 9 replace peony with the alternative selection—white Jupiter's-beard—and choose other alternative selections if you'd like to. In dry-summer zone 10, use all the alternative selections.

Pruning and general cleanup in late winter or early spring constitute the major annual maintenance for this garden. Remove old, unproductive wood from the mock orange and rose, then prune only if you need to correct their shape or limit their size. Cut the Russian sage and catmint to the ground; cut back the English lavender by half. Most perennials will need periodic dividing and replanting after three or four years. However, you many need to replace the beardtongue, border penstemon, mallow, and golden feverfew as frequently as every other year.

Variations

This kidney-shaped bed was designed as an island planting to ornament an expanse of lawn; the low plants at the perimeter scale up to the two high points of mock orange and shrub rose. If you draw a line through the bed connecting the dots shown on both ends of the plan, you will create two irregular beds either of which you could place against a fence or wall. The half-oval bed will contain two high points: the shrub rose and the mock orange; the serpentine-edge bed will gain its height from the mock orange.

Hemerocallis 'Knob Hill' (daylily)

Pastel-Shades Garden Plants

A. *Philadelphus × virginalis* 'Minnesota Snowflake' (mock orange) (2)
B. *Rosa* 'Pink Meidilland' or 'Bonica' (2)
C. *Potentilla ×* 'Katherine Dykes' (cinquefoil) (2)
D. *Perovskia atriplicifolia* (Russian sage) (7)
E. *Lythrum salicaria* 'Morden's Pink' (loosestrife) (5)
F. *Paeonia lactiflora*, white cultivar (peony) (2)
G. *Dictamnus albus* (gasplant) (4)
H. *Monarda didyma* 'Croftway Pink' (beebalm) (7)
I. *Hemerocallis*, light yellow miniature cultivar (daylily) (4)
J. *Hemerocallis*, light pink cultivar (daylily) (8)
K. *Achillea ×* 'Moonshine' (yarrow) (14)
L. *Gypsophila paniculata* 'Viette's Dwarf' (baby's-breath) (2)
M. *Penstemon barbatus* 'Rose Elf' (beardtongue) (11)
N. *Aster × frikartii* (aster) (11)
O. *Geranium endressii* 'Wargrave Pink' (cranesbill) (12)
P. *Stachys byzantina* (lamb's-ears) (9)
Q. *Geranium sanguineum* (cranesbill) (2)
R. *Lavandula angustifolia* 'Munstead' (English lavender) (7)
S. *Monarda didyma* 'Violet Queen' (beebalm) (9)
T. *Nepeta × faassenii* (catmint) (11)
U. *Chrysanthemem parthenium* 'Aureum' (golden feverfew) (5)
V. *Malva alcea* var. *fastigiata* (mallow) (7)

Alternative Selections

A. *Buddleia davidii*, white cultivar (common butterflybush) (2)
C. *Chrysanthemum frutescens*, yellow (marguerite) (2)
D. *Lavandula angustifolia* (English lavender) (7)
F. *Centranthus ruber* 'Albus' (white Jupiter's-beard) (4)
G. *Baptisia australis* (false-indigo) (2)
H. *Echinacea purpurea*, white cultivar (purple coneflower) (7)
L. *Artemisia arborescens* (artemisia) (1)
M. *Penstemon × gloxinioides* (border penstemon) (11)
Q. *Nierembergia hippomanica* var. *violacea* (dwarf cupflower) (2)
S. *Felicia amelloides* (blue marguerite) (6)

Lythrum salicaria (loosestrife)

Paeonia lactiflora (peony)

Hemerocallis

Aster

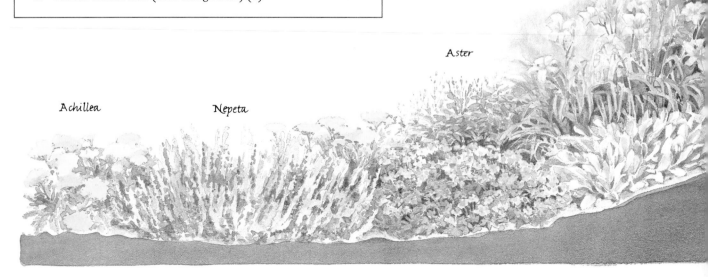

Achillea   *Nepeta*

Pastel-Shades Garden

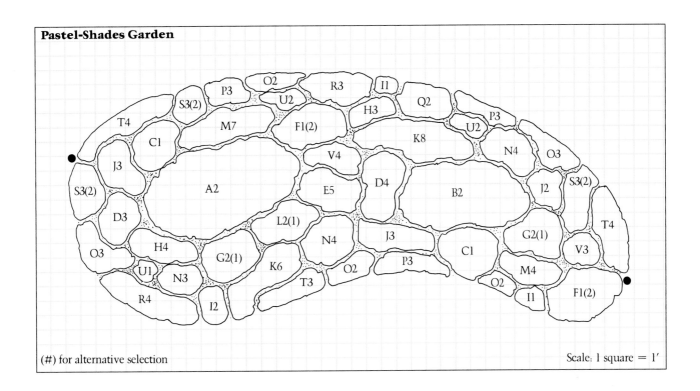

(#) for alternative selection

Scale: 1 square = 1'

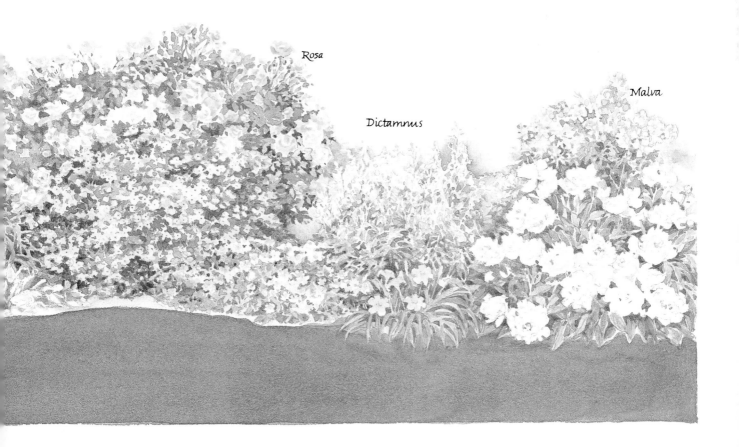

Rosa

Malva

Dictamnus

A HOT AND BRIGHT GARDEN

This bed fairly shouts, "Hey, look at me," though dark glasses might be in order. Red, orange, and yellow jostle for attention, punctuated by patches of vibrant purple. The perennials (and annuals on the alternative list) reach their brassy climax appropriately in summer and, weather permitting, will last into fall. Much of this brightness is provided by those mainstays of summer: members of the daisy family. Aside from the roses, which give color from spring into fall, all the plants are perennials. For a planting scheme that features summer annuals, use the list of alternative selections.

This vibrant garden bed needs as much sun as possible—the bright colors, sunshine, and summer warmth combine to create a scene that radiates. The main plant list is suitable for zones 4 through 9 and dry-summer zone 10. The alternative selections are annuals for the same zones, although the gazanias and gaillardias may not be at their best where the summers are hot and wet.

In zones 4 through 7, maintenance begins in fall when you will need to protect the roses from lethal winter temperatures. The two standard roses are particularly vulnerable and will need special attention (see Ortho's book *All*

About Roses). In all zones, late winter or early spring is the time to prune the roses, to remove weak and worn out wood and to shape the plants. Perennials should get an annual cleanup: remove the dead leaves and spent stems in fall or in early spring before growth begins. In zones 4 through 7, you will need to replace the penstemons and dahlias each year; the other perennials will need dividing and replanting periodically as they become overcrowded. If you plant any of the annuals from the alternative selections, you will need to replace them every spring.

Variations

You can cut the length of the bed by one third if you draw a line between the two dots shown on the plan and eliminate all the plants in the smaller portion. The number of Goldfink core-

Rosa

Hemerocallis

Salvia

Rudbeckia

Rudbeckia hirta (black-eyed-susan)

opsis will be cut to four and the alternative purple scarlet sage will be cut to eight. To make a better edge where the line has shortened the bed, plant five gaillardias, instead of the butterfly weed, three sundrops instead of the common yarrow, and four sage plants instead of the penstemon. If you are using the alternative list, substitute 12 French marigolds for the African marigolds, 2 zinnias for the common yarrow, and 5 gazanias for the penstemon.

Rosa 'Redgold'

Hemerocallis 'New Yorker' (daylily)

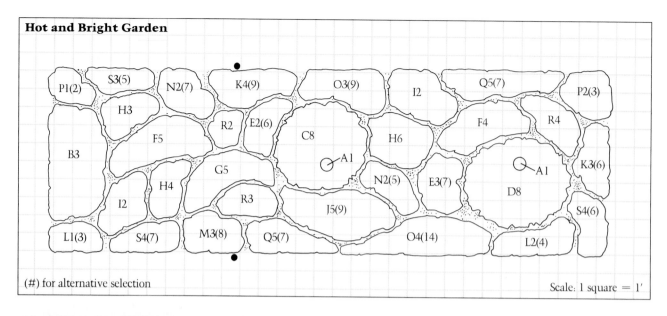

Hot and Bright Garden

P1(2)   S3(5)   N2(7)   K4(9)   O3(9)   I2   Q5(7)   P2(3)

H3   R2   E2(6)   F4   R4

F5   C8   H6

B3   A1   A1   K3(6)

G5   N2(5)   E3(7)   D8

H4   R3   J5(9)   S4(6)

I2

L1(3)   S4(7)   M3(8)   Q5(7)   O4(14)   L2(4)

(#) for alternative selection   Scale: 1 square = 1′

Gazania (gazania)

Coreopsis lanceolata 'Goldfink' (coreopsis)

Hot and Bright Garden Plants
A. *Rosa* 'Redgold', standard ("tree") (2)
B. *Rosa* 'Europeana' (3)
C. *Hemerocallis*, yellow cultivar (daylily) (8)
D. *Hemerocallis*, red cultivar (daylily) (8)
E. *Asclepias tuberosa* (butterfly weed) (5)
F. *Achillea filipendulina* 'Coronation Gold' (fernleaf yarrow) (9)
G. *Achillea millefolium* 'Fire King' (common yarrow) (5)
H. *Rudbeckia hirta* (black-eyed-susan) (13)
I. *Anthemis tinctoria* (golden marguerite) (4)
J. *Coreopsis lanceolata* 'Brown Eyes' (coreopsis) (5)
K. *Coreopsis lanceolata* 'Goldfink' (coreopsis) (7)
L. *Coreopsis verticillata* 'Zagreb' (coreopsis) (3)
M. *Coreopsis auriculata* 'Nana' (coreopsis) (3)
N. *Helenium autumnale* 'Brilliant' (common sneezeweed) (4)
O. *Gaillardia* × *grandiflora* 'Baby Cole' (gaillardia) (7)
P. *Oenothera fruticosa* (sundrops) (3)
Q. *Dahlia*, bedding type, preferably red or orange flowers (10)
R. *Penstemon* × *gloxinioides,* purple cultivar (9)
S. *Salvia* × *superba* (sage) (11)

Alternative Selections
E. *Tagetes erecta*, yellow selection (African marigold) (13)
J. *Zinnia grandiflora*, orange selection (zinnia) (9)
K. *Salvia splendens*, purple selection (purple scarlet sage) (15)
L. *Gaillardia pulchella* 'Lorenziana' (gaillardia) (7)
M. *Gazania*, yellow cultivar (gazania) (8)
N. *Nicotiana alata*, red selection (flowering tobacco) (12)
O. *Tagetes patula* (French marigold) (23)
P. *Zinnia angustifolia* (zinnia) (5)
Q. *Salvia splendens*, red selection (scarlet sage) (14)
S. *Gazania*, orange cultivar (gazania) (18)

A COLORFUL FOLIAGE GARDEN

Most gardens rely on flowers for color. This planting scheme gives a different color angle: your chance to say it with foliage. A few of the plants do bear blossoms, but the floral show is merely a dividend in a planting that will be a colorful tapestry of leaves from spring through fall. There is even one green-leafed plant—the germander—in the design, included as an exotic and colorful counterpoint to the reds, yellows, and grays.

With one exception, this planting will thrive in zones 5 through 9, given well-drained soil, and sun for at least six hours each day. The golden elderberry needs more winter chill than zones 8 and 9 can offer. In these zones, choose golden elaeagnus from the alternative selections. Gardeners in dry-summer zone 10 should choose all the alternative selections—the golden elaeagnus instead of the golden elderberry, the dusty-miller instead of the Russian sage, the kalanchoe instead of the redleaf Japanese barberry, and the golden feverfew instead of the spiraea. The alternative selections can also be used in zone 9.

Once-a-year maintenance should keep this planting presentable. In late winter or early spring, do some general cleanup and pruning. Cut back the Russian sage, catmint, and eulalia-grass to within a few inches of the ground. Cut back the English lavender and tricolor garden sage by about half to promote compact growth. As necessary—perhaps not yearly—cut back the lavender-cotton and germander to keep them compact. Thin the oldest, unproductive stems from the spiraea; if necessary, head back to shape the Vicary golden privet and golden elderberry. After several years the stonecrop may start to become patchy. When this happens, fill in the bare spots with new cuttings or replant entirely with new cuttings or plants.

Variations

For a smaller bed, you can use only two thirds of the plan—going as far as, and including, the redleaf Japanese barberry, but stopping short of the golden elderberry. If you need a straight back line, extend the existing back line to the edge of the bed, eliminating the catmint planting and one plant of the lavender-cotton.

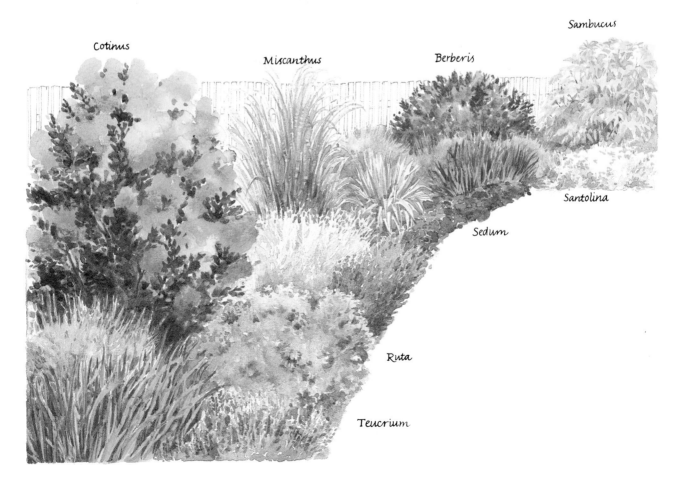

Sambucus

Cotinus

Miscanthus

Berberis

Santolina

Sedum

Ruta

Teucrium

Colorful-Foliage Garden Plants

A. *Cotinus coggygria* 'Royal Purple' (smoke tree) (1)
B. *Ligustrum × vicaryi* (Vicary golden privet) (1)
C. *Sambucus racemosa* 'Plumosa Aurea' (golden elderberry) (1)
D. *Perovskia atriplicifolia* (Russian sage) (3)
E. *Yucca filamentosa* 'Gold Sword' or 'Bright Eagle' (1)
F. *Berberis thunbergii* 'Atropurpurea' (redleaf Japanese barberry) (1)
G. *Lavandula angustifolia* (English lavender) (6)
H. *Ruta graveolens* 'Jackman's Blue' (rue) (2)
I. *Imperata cylindrica* 'Rubra' (Japanese bloodgrass) (7)
J. *Santolina chamaecyparissus* (lavender-cotton) (9)
K. *Teucrium chamaedrys* (germander) (5)
L. *Sedum spurium* 'Dragon's Blood' (stonecrop) (8)
M. *Salvia officinalis* 'Tricolor' (tricolor garden sage) (5)
N. *Miscanthus sinensis* (eulalia-grass) (2)
O. *Nepeta × faassenii* (catmint) (4)
P. *Spiraea × bumalda* 'Limemound' (spiraea) (1)
Q. *Molinia caerulea* 'Variegata' (variegated moorgrass) (1)

Alternative Selections

C. *Elaeagnus pungens* 'Maculata' (golden elaeagnus) (1)
D. *Senecio vira-vira, S. cineraria* 'Candissimus', or *S. leucostachys* (dusty-miller) (3)
F. *Kalanchoe laciniata* (Christmas tree kalanchoe) (1)
P. *Chrysanthemum parthenium* 'Aureum' (golden feverfew) (2)

Santolina chamaecyparissus (lavender-cotton)

Berberis thunbergii 'Atropurpurea' (redleaf Japanese barberry)

Colorful Foliage Garden

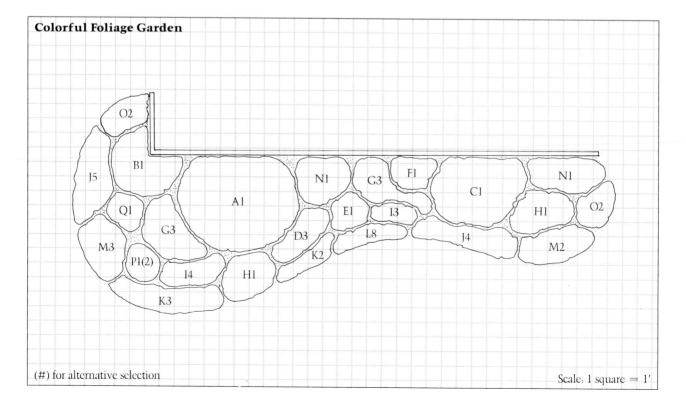

(#) for alternative selection

Scale: 1 square = 1'

Cornus
Elaeagnus
Hippophae
Festuca
Thymus
Santolina
Helictotrichon

A GRAY GARDEN

Soothing, misty, and even ghostly, this gray garden features subtle contrasts of foliage tones, shapes, and textures. Leaves range in color from gray-green and silvery blue to almost white, and vary in shape from broad to narrow, from simple to filigree to spiky. Even the leaf surfaces play a part; some are almost furry and others are covered with a delicate plumlike bloom. Depending on foliage and habit of growth, the effect of each plant varies from solid and bulky to intricately twiggy to feathery. All this subtle interplay is made for close-up viewing—and best appreciated from an appropriately gray bench of concrete or weathered wood.

Despite a color scheme suggesting fog or overcast skies, this garden prefers sun for at least six hours a day. In hot-summer regions, though, the dogwood (and alternative hydrangea) will benefit from some afternoon shading by the Russian olive (or the alternative weeping willow-leaved pear). Given insufficient shade, the dogwood and hydrangea will be the first shrubs to show signs of water stress. Most of the plants will prosper with a little less water than that provided by routine garden watering, but they do need well-drained soil—especially the gray-leafed perennials, which may die in wet winter soils. The main list plants thrive in zones 6 through 8. In zone 9 and dry-summer zone 10, choose the alternative selections.

Some late winter or early spring pruning should be a yearly maintenance ritual. Remove the old stems of the dogwood or hydrangea, and cut back the remaining stems as needed to shape the plants or control their size. Cut the blue-mist, Russian sage, and catmint to within a few inches of the ground. Cut back by about half the artemisias and English lavender. To keep the plants shapely, head back wayward stems of the sea-buckthorn and silverberry, or the bush germander and variegated tobira, and trim back or shear the lavender-cotton whenever it exceeds its boundaries. The crown-pink is a biennial or short-lived perennial, but reseeds easily; keep young plants coming along as replacements. Divide and replant the lamb's-ears and snow-in-summer after several years or whenever they begin to thin out and appear untidy. Divide and replant the iris every three or four years.

Variations

You can make this planting smaller and rectangular if you extend the straight edge that starts at the corner planting of blue oatgrass. This will give you a smaller crescent of paving stones and thyme, and will put the total number of blue fescue to five and Russian sage to two.

Gray Garden

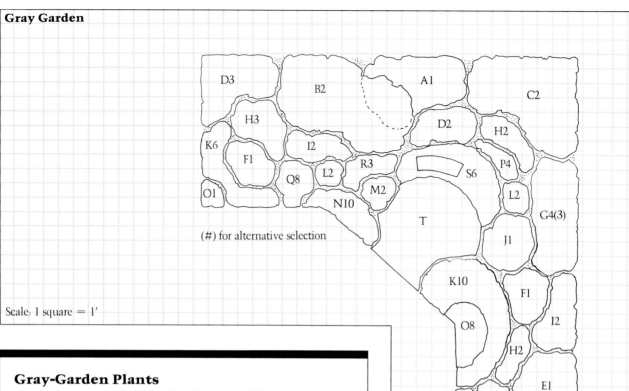

(#) for alternative selection

Scale: 1 square = 1'

Gray-Garden Plants

A. *Elaeagnus angustifolia* (Russian olive) (1)
B. *Cornus alba* 'Elegantissima' (variegated Tatarian dogwood) (2)
C. *Hippophae rhamnoides* (sea-buckthorn) (2)
D. *Caryopteris* × *clandonensis* (blue-mist) (5)
E. *Elaeagnus commutata* (silverberry) (1)
F. *Ruta graveolens* 'Jackman's Blue' (rue) (3)
G. *Perovskia atriplicifolia* (Russian sage) (4)
H. *Lavandula angustifolia* (English lavender) (7)
I. *Echinops exaltatus* (globethistle) (4)
J. *Artemisia* × 'Powis Castle' (1)
K. *Santolina chamaecyparissus* (lavender-cotton) (16)
L. *Iris*, tall bearded hybrid 'Song of Norway' (4)
M. *Nepeta* × *faassenii* (catmint) (8)
N. *Festuca ovina* var. *glauca* (blue fescue) (10)
O. *Helictotrichon sempervirens* (blue oatgrass) (9)
P. *Stachys byzantina* (lamb's-ears) (4)
Q. *Lychnis coronaria* 'Alba' (crown-pink) (8)
R. *Artemisia stellerana* (beach wormwood) (3)
S. *Cerastium tomentosum* (snow-in-summer) (6)
T. *Thymus pseudolanuginosus* (woolly thyme) (number depends on pattern of paving stones)

Alternative Selections

A. *Pyrus salicifolia* 'Pendula' (weeping willow-leaved pear) (1)
B. *Hydrangea macrophylla* 'Tricolor' (bigleaf hydrangea) (2)
C. *Teucrium fruticans* (bush germander) (2)
D. *Convolvulus cneorum* (bush morning glory) (5)
E. *Pittosporum tobira* 'Variegata' (variegated tobira) (1)
G. *Salvia leucophylla* (purple sage) (3)

Helictotrichon sempervirens (blue oatgrass)

AN ENGLISH COTTAGE GARDEN

To suggest a design for a cottage garden is something of a contradiction. Original cottage gardens arose not from plans or preconceived notions but fairly haphazardly, according to the needs and desires of the gardener and the plants available. A typical example contained an apparently random assortment of ornamentals and even some edibles, a mix of shrubs, perennials, and annuals. The original cottage garden was a colorful assortment of plants presented in a homey disarray—sometimes with clear pathways, sometimes without.

This plan captures the essence of a cottage garden but organizes the varied plants along both sides of a pathway—a scheme that could be used easily in any rectangular yard. The path need not be straight, but the surface should be as natural looking as possible: gravel, decomposed granite, crazy paving with spaces for thyme between the stones—or even ground bark. Flowering in this garden starts in spring and continues into fall, reaching a peak in late spring to mid-summer.

You can recreate this cottage garden in zones 5 through 9 in any space that receives full sun. The list of alternative plants suggests substitutes for zone 9 that also will extend into dry-summer zone 10. Be sure you give the planting routine garden watering.

The happy hodgepodge that is a cottage garden needs considerable maintenance just before the growing season. Clean up dead perennial leaves and stems from last year's growth; divide and replant any perennials that are overcrowded, except for the iris, which you should reset in summer. Replace any short-lived perennials that have shown signs of decline. Cut back the blue-mist to within several inches of the ground. When the soil warms, set out the cosmos and love-in-a-mist. The flowering shrubs—roses and spiraea—bloom in spring, so heading them back hard when they are dormant will remove potential blossoms. While they are dormant, prune only to remove dead and old, unproductive wood. Throughout the flowering season, remove the spent blooms whenever they become unsightly. After the shrubs have finished blooming, you can prune them to control their size.

Variations

Although the charm of a cottage garden is fully appreciated only when you can stroll among the plants, you can use either half of this plan as an individual border—one deep, one narrow. You may lose a little of the cottage mood, but at least you will retain the friendly jumble of plants. If you choose to plant only the narrow border, you might prefer to install a bench instead of the sundial.

Dianthus plumarius (cottage pink)

Chrysanthemum

Alcea

Rosa

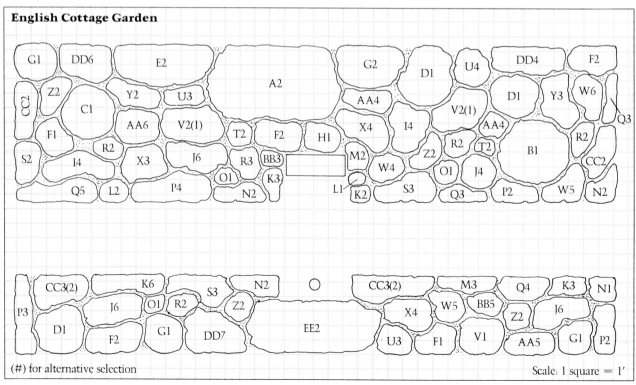

English Cottage Garden

(#) for alternative selection

Scale: 1 square = 1′

Alcea

Lilium

Achillea filipendulina (fernleaf yarrow)

English Cottage–Garden Plants

A. *Rosa* 'Alba Maxima' (2)
B. *Rosa hugonis* (Father Hugo's rose) (1)
C. *Spiraea thunbergii* (spiraea) (1)
D. *Paeonia lactiflora*, pink cultivar, such as 'Mons. Jules Elie' (peony) (3)
E. *Caryopteris* × *clandonensis* (blue-mist) (2)
F. *Lavandula angustifolia* (English lavender) (8)
G. *Perovskia atriplicifolia* (Russian sage) (5)
H. *Potentilla* × 'Katherine Dykes' (cinquefoil) (1)
I. *Lupinus* Russell hybrids (Russell lupine) (8)
J. *Chrysanthemum* × *superbum* 'Polaris' (Shasta daisy) (22)
K. *Dianthus plumarius*, any cultivar (cottage pink) (14)
L. *Iris* 'Pallida Variegata' (3)
M. *Iberis sempervirens* (evergreen candytuft) (5)
N. *Cerastium tomentosum* (snow-in-summer) (7)
O. *Hemerocallis flava* (*H. lilioasphodelus*) (lemon daylily) (3)
P. *Nepeta* × *faassenii* (catmint) (11)
Q. *Stachys byzantina* (lamb's-ears) (15)
R. *Phlox carolina* 'Miss Lingard' (thickleaf phlox) (11)
S. *Geranium endressii* 'Wargrave Pink' (cranesbill) (8)
T. *Lilium regale* (regal lily) (4)
U. *Alcea rosea* (hollyhock) (10)
V. *Gypsophila paniculata* 'Bristol Fairy' (baby's-breath) (5)
W. *Lychnis coronaria* (crown-pink) (20)
X. *Aster* × *frikartii* (aster) (11)
Y. *Aster novi-belgii*, pink or red cultivar (New York aster) (5)
Z. *Campanula persicifolia* (peachleaf bluebell) (8)
AA. *Cosmos bipinnatus* (cosmos) (19)
BB. *Nigella damascena* (love-in-a-mist) (8)
CC. *Alchemilla mollis* (lady's-mantle) (10)
DD. *Achillea filipendulina* 'Gold Plate' or 'Coronation Gold' (fernleaf yarrow) (17)
EE. *Rosa gallica* 'Versicolor' ('Rosa Mundi') (2)

Alternative Selections

C. *Cistus* × 'Doris Hibberson' (rockrose) (1)
D. *Mirabilis jalapa* (four-o'clock) (3)
E. *Salvia leucantha* (Mexican bush sage) (2)
H. *Anthemis tinctoria* (golden marguerite) (1)
I. *Centranthus ruber* (Jupiter's-beard) (8)
R. *Agapanthus orientalis* 'Albidus' (white lily-of-the-Nile) (11)
V. *Chrysanthemum frutescens* (marguerite) (3)
CC. *Coreopsis verticillata* 'Moonbeam' (coreopsis) (8)

A JAPANESE GARDEN

The Japanese garden is a highly evolved art form that aims to capture the essence of nature's landscapes in the confines of a garden. Success is a question of choosing particular plants, carefully training and pruning them, and using certain elements as surrogates for portions of the natural landscape—for example, rocks to represent mountains or hills. The more fortunately sited Japanese gardens borrow scenic elements from beyond the garden, such as a hillside or mountain, as backdrops to increase the illusion of space and distance. Others turn inward, becoming jewel-like microcosms within their boundaries. This Japanese scheme is of the latter, self-contained sort, with boundary fencing (perhaps of weathered wood) on three sides. It would work well as a patio garden with a paved surface leading up to the front edges.

Certain plants are inseparably associated with Japanese gardens: azaleas, bamboos, pines, and Japanese maples, to name a few. Unfortunately, a number of these key plants are broad-leaved evergreens that are impossible to grow in zones 3 to 7. The main plant list for this garden will work in zones 6 through 8, except for the dwarf heavenly-bamboo, which is not reliably hardy in zones 6 and 7. For these colder zones there is no low-growing bamboo-like substitute, so plant the alternative selection—Japanese barberry—which at least provides a fine texture. Gardeners in zones 9 and 10, where real cold tolerance is not an issue, can plant the dwarf heavenly-bamboo, but otherwise should use the alternative selections. The plants for this garden need good light but not necessarily full sun for the entire day; four to six hours of sun will suffice.

A Japanese garden needs ongoing maintenance but nothing major at any one time. Just before the growing season starts, clean up the dead growth of the previous year. Trim ground cover plants—the junipers and Japanese spurge, or alternative sweet box—if they are expanding beyond their limits; head back the dwarf heavenly-bamboo and cotoneaster if you need to control their height or spread. Prune or shape the flowering shrubs—azalea and rhododendron, or India hawthorn—just after flowering finishes. During the growing season, remove wayward growth on plants that are overrunning their allotted spaces or departing from the shapes you intend. Throughout the year, keep the planting free of dead leaves, flowers, and other litter.

Variations

Because a garden in Japanese style is conceived as an individual scene, it can't be altered in size without losing essential parts; therefore, smaller or larger gardens usually require different designs. You can, however, simplify this scheme by changing the smaller pool to a raked sand bed; if you do this, you won't, of course, need the water plant, the variegated sweet flag.

Japanese-Garden Plants

A. *Magnolia stellata* (star magnolia) (1)
B. *Acer palmatum* (Japanese maple) (1)
C. *Cotoneaster apiculatus* (cranberry cotoneaster) (3)
D. *Juniperus chinensis* 'Blue Vase' (Texas star juniper) (1)
E. *Pinus mugo* var. *mugo* (mugo pine) (1)
F. *Rhododendron*, Kaempferi hybrid, such as 'Fedora' or 'John Cairns' (azalea) (6)
G. *Rhododendron yakusimanum* (3)
H. *Nandina domestica* 'Harbour Dwarf' (dwarf heavenly-bamboo) (3)
I. *Juniperus sabina* 'Blue Danube' (juniper) (2)
J. *Juniperus horizontalis* 'Wiltonii' (juniper) (2)
K. *Liriope spicata* (creeping lily-turf) (29)
L. *Hosta sieboldiana* (*H. glauca*) (plantain lily) (4)
M. *Acorus gramineus* 'Variegatus' (variegated sweet flag) (3)
N. *Iris pseudacorus* (yellow flag) (1)
O. *Pachysandra terminalis* (Japanese spurge) (20)
P. *Imperata cylindrica* 'Rubra' ('Red Baron') (Japanese bloodgrass) (9)
Q. *Anemone* × *hybrida* 'Honorine Jobert' (Japanese anemone) (8)
R. *Bergenia crassifolia* (winter-blooming bergenia) (10)
S. *Ajuga reptans* (carpet-bugle) (10)
T. *Sagina subulata* or *Arenaria verna* (Irish moss) (several flats: 2-inch squares cut and planted 6 inches apart)

Alternative Selections

F. *Rhododendron*, Kurume hybrid, such as 'Hinodegiri' or 'Hino-Crimson' (azalea) (6)
G. *Raphiolepis indica* 'Ballerina' (India-hawthorn) (3)
H. *Berberis thunbergii* 'Crimson Pygmy', for zones 6 and 7 (Japanese barberry) (3)
K. *Ophiopogon japonicus* (mondograss) (29)
L. *Helleborus orientalis* (Lenten-rose) (4)
O. *Sarcococca hookerana* var. *humilis* (sweet box) (8)

Magnolia

Rhododendron
kaempferi

Rhododendron
yakusimanum

Liriope

Japanese Garden

F5

G1

E1

T

C3

Q8

O11(4)

T

A1

K7

J2

F1

B1

P4

Sand

K8

O9(4)

H3

M1

G1

N1

K5

D1

S10

P5

R3

L4

M1

K9

T

G1

M1

R4

I2

R3

(#) for alternative selection

Scale: 1 square = 1'

A VICTORIAN CARPET-BEDDING GARDEN

The Victorian penchant for elaborate ornamentation extended even into the garden. Borrowing from the older traditions of parterres and knots, and working with an assortment of colorful annuals, Victorian gardeners developed a planting style that evoked both the richness and intricacy of Persian carpets—hence the term *carpet bedding*. Think of this garden as a sort of knot garden (see pages 46 to 47) untied. In place of rigidly controlled lines and curves within a square frame, carpet-bedding design introduced flowing curves, loops, and even heraldic-style decorative motifs executed in low-growing flowering and foliage plants.

Many of the most impressive Victorian examples of carpet bedding were executed on a grand scale: circles, ovals, or squares set in lawns of estates and municipal parks; long curving or rectangular beds bordering public and private drives. A typical bedding scheme employed a repeated design, and often an exotic centerpiece such as a palm or yucca. This bedding plan incorporates both of these features. The garden is small but expandable and reasonably simple to lay out, especially if you mark the design on bare earth with a sprinkling of flour or gypsum.

Place this garden where it will receive sun all day. A surrounding lawn nicely sets off the colorful floral tapestry, but other contexts may be just as attractive. Give the garden regular watering: Its effectiveness depends on continual flower production. Because this colorful carpet is made from annuals and plants treated as annuals, it is suitable for all zones. The alternative list provides a different color scheme featuring yellow, white, and blue. You will need to replant the annuals each spring, but you can keep the potted accent plant year after year if you heed its limit of cold tolerance. Either choose one adapted to your zone or move a tender specimen indoors for the winter.

Each spring you need to start maintenance literally from the ground up. Remove last year's spent plants, rework the soil, lay out the design, then set out new plants when the soil has warmed. During the growing season, the garden will need grooming.

Variations

The bed design contains one central circle connected to circles at either end. You can extend the length by adding further circles and connecting "ribbons" within the bed, repeating the design, and ending the bed as illustrated. With a little calculation, you can even bend an extended planting into a crescent-shaped bed. You can also vary the planting by choosing different color selections or by choosing different plants from the alternative selections.

Victorian Carpet-Bedding Plants

A. *Begonia* × *semperflorens-cultorum*, red-foliaged selection (wax begonia) (96)
B. *Centaurea cineraria* (dusty-miller) (64)
C. *Verbena* × *hybrida*, red selection (garden verbena) (115)
D. *Lobularia maritima*, white selection (sweet alyssum) (56)
E. *Pelargonium* × *hortorum*, red selection (common geranium) (15)
F. *Salvia splendens*, red selection (scarlet sage) (30)
G. *Centaurea cineraria* (dusty-miller) (18)
H. Accent plant in pot, such as *Cordyline australis* (grass palm), *Cycas revoluta* (sago palm), *Phormium tenax* (New Zealand flax), *Strelitzia reginae* (bird-of-paradise), or *Yucca filamentosa* (Adam's needle) or *Y. flaccida* (1)

Alternative Selections

A. *Tagetes patula*, yellow selection (French marigold) (96)
B. *Begonia* × *semperflorens-cultorum*, white selection (wax begonia) (90)
C. *Petunia* × *hybrida*, blue selection (petunia) (115)
E. *Pelargonium* × *hortorum*, white selection (common geranium) (15)
F. *Tagetes*, yellow-flowered triploid hybrid (triploid marigold) (30)

Tagetes (marigold)

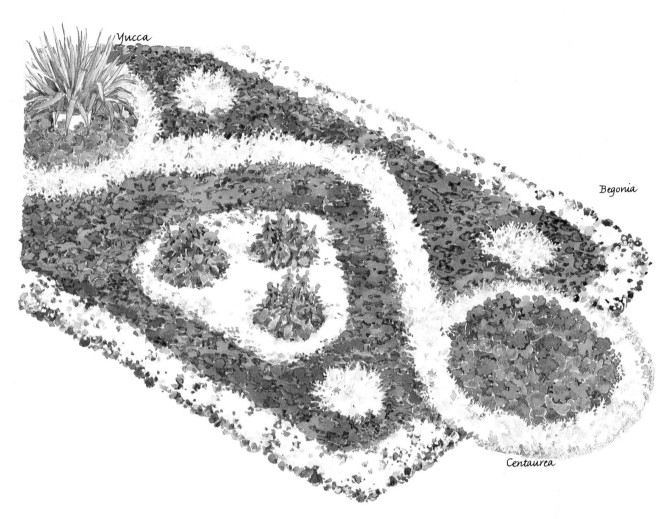

Yucca

Begonia

Centaurea

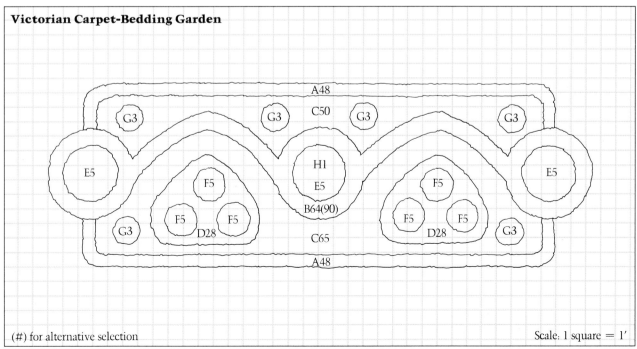

Victorian Carpet-Bedding Garden

A48

G3   G3   C50   G3   G3

E5   F5   H1   F5   E5

E5

G3   F5   F5   B64(90)   F5   F5   G3

D28   C65   D28

A48

(#) for alternative selection   Scale: 1 square = 1'

A KNOT GARDEN

From purely utilitarian beginnings in medieval times, gardening in western Europe took an increasingly decorative tack during the Renaissance. A vogue for clipped hedging and topiary work culminated in elaborate parterres and, in the sixteenth and seventeenth centuries, the knot garden—a square garden containing a geometric ribbonlike interweaving of dwarf clipped hedges around accent plants. In each knot, the spaces between the ribbons would be filled with herbs, flowers, or colored pebbles. A

zone 10. For a more colorful knot, consider alternative selections, which thrive in the same zones. The alternative plants also fall in the herb category, though the calendulas are almost universally grown as bedding annuals.

An attractive knot garden depends on crisp edges, and this means frequent trimming. During the growing season, give the hedges a light haircut every week or two. And perhaps periodically trim the herbs to keep them within their assigned boundaries and to maintain somewhat uniform surfaces. Plants on both

Santolina virens

Origanum

Lavandula

Teucrium

Santolina chamaecyparissus

basic knot garden contained four such knots, separated by pathways.

Many knot patterns contained arcs, circles, and elaborate curlicues. The pattern presented here uses straight lines, designed for simple execution. The plants on the main list are a traditional variety of herbs, all of which will grow in zones 5 through 9 and dry-summer

lists need full sun. The plants on the main list are perennials or small shrubs, all of which will live for a number of years with moderate watering (they can take some dryness between waterings). Especially where summer rainfall is the rule, be sure to give the plants well-drained soil. Among the alternative plants, the calendulas must be planted anew each year.

Variations

As long as you retain the precise interlacing ribbons of clipped plants, you can work countless variations on a knot garden by changing the plant selections. For the hedge plants you need only something that will not grow big, has small foliage, and can be closely clipped. A later tradition used boxwood (*Buxus sempervirens*) exclusively; this retained the essential geometry of the style though it lost the interweaving appearance of different foliages.

There are numerous possibilities for the hedges. You could use boxwood interwoven with dwarf redleaf Japanese barberry (*Berberis thunbergii* 'Crimson Pygmy'). In the cool-summer regions of zones 7, 8, and 9, you could interweave hedges of heaths (*Erica*) or heathers (*Calluna*) in contrasting foliage colors. Choices for the spaces between the ribbons are truly far ranging. Imagine a knot planted with a single sweep of dwarf marigolds, zinnias, or petunias!

Knot Garden

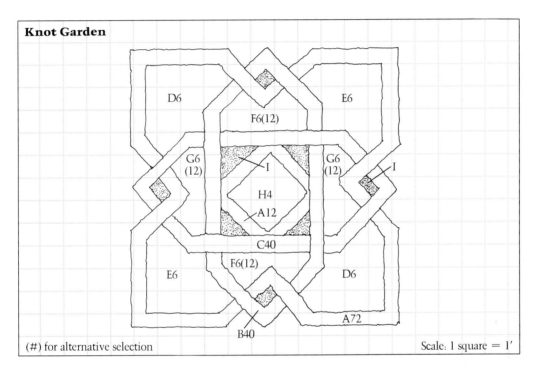

D6   E6

F6(12)

G6 (12)   G6 (12)   I

I

H4
A12

C40

F6(12)

E6   D6

A72

B40

(#) for alternative selection   Scale: 1 square = 1'

Calendula officinalis (pot marigold)

Knot-Garden Plants

A. *Teucrium chamaedrys* (germander) (84)
B. *Santolina chamaecyparissus* (lavender-cotton) (40)
C. *Santolina virens* (green santolina) (40)
D. *Salvia officinalis* 'Tricolor' (tricolor garden sage) (12)
E. *Salvia officinalis* 'Icterina' (variegated garden sage) (12)
F. *Hyssopus officinalis* (hyssop) (12)
G. *Origanum majorana* (sweet marjoram) (12)
H. *Lavandula angustifolia* 'Munstead' (English lavender) (4)
I. Gravel or crushed rocks

Alternative Selections

D. *Thymus* × *citriodorus* (lemon thyme) (12)
E. *Thymus vulgaris* 'Argenteus' (silver thyme) (12)
F. *Calendula officinalis*, dwarf cream selection (pot marigold) (24)
G. *Calendula officinalis*, dwarf yellow selection (pot marigold) (24)

A ROCK GARDEN

In its most sophisticated form, a rock garden recreates the above-timberline, rock-strewn landscape as a garden for choice, culturally demanding alpine plants. At its other, most casual extreme, the rock garden may be a dry-set stone retaining wall embellished with various prostrate annuals, perennials, and succulents that find rootholds in the crevices. Many rock-gardening enthusiasts, other than alpine-plant specialists, practice an art that lies somewhere between the two extremes, making gardens that skillfully mingle rocks and small plants in a naturalistic manner.

This rock-garden plan features easy-to-grow shrubs and perennials, all of which have reputations as good rock-garden subjects because of their sizes and growth habits. Plants in the main list will thrive in a sunny location in zones 5 through 8 where summers are humid and in zones 5 through 9 where summers are fairly dry. Gardeners in dry-summer zone 10 should substitute plants from the alternative selections; gardeners in dry-summer zone 9 may use plants from either list. In all zones give the plants well-drained soil and regular watering. Although the rock-garden plan is shown as a ground-level garden surrounded by pathways, you might want to use the same plan for a raised garden or even as a planting on a gentle slope.

Because you won't be able to find rocks that exactly match the sizes or configurations indicated, you should consider the plan a general guide rather than a blueprint. Use it as a key to harmonious plant associations and as an illustration of natural-appearing rock groupings. When you are selecting rocks, choose those native to your area if possible. Local rocks will look the most natural. Always try to set rocks as they would appear in nature. A garden of craggy, miniature Matterhorns, for example, will always look artificial.

Maintaining a rock garden is an ongoing exercise in tidying. Never is there a great amount of labor at one time, but neglected edges show clearly. Begin in late winter or early spring by removing dead leaves and old flowering stems, then assess the condition of the plants. Lightly head back or shear spreading shrubs and perennials that are overgrowing their bounds. Replace any shorter-lived perennials (such as evergreen candytuft) that have remained sparse or patchy after last year's trimming. During the growing season, remove spent flowers as they fade.

Variations

Remembering that this planting scheme is a general guide rather than a blueprint, you can vary the garden's dimensions and size to suit your space and assortment of rocks. All the plants except the conifers and shrubs are low growing, with the very lowest-profile individuals at the perimeter of the garden. If you alter the size of the plan, use the perimeter plants to finish off the edges.

Rock-Garden Plants

A. *Chamaecyparis obtusa* 'Nana' (dwarf Hinoki cypress) (1)
B. *Platycladus orientalis* 'Bonita' (Oriental arborvitae) (1)
C. *Calluna vulgaris* 'J.H. Hamilton' (heather) or *Erica carnea* 'Springwood' (heath) (2)
D. *Berberis thunbergii* 'Crimson Pygmy' (Japanese barberry) (2)
E. *Helianthemum nummularium* (sun-rose) (3)
F. *Thymus pseudolanuginosus* (woolly thyme) (5)
G. *Sempervivum tectorum* (hen-and-chickens) (6)
H. *Oenothera missourensis* (evening primrose) (3)
I. *Phlox subulata* (moss pink) (2)
J. *Iberis sempervirens* (evergreen candytuft) (4)
K. *Arabis caucasica* (wall rockcress) (5)
L. *Aurinia saxatilis* (basket-of-gold) (3)
M. *Dianthus* × 'Tiny Rubies' (pink) (4)
N. *Dianthus* × 'Rose Bowl' (pink) (5)
O. *Saponaria ocymoides* (soapwort) (1)
P. *Imperata cylindrica* 'Rubra' (Japanese bloodgrass) (3)
Q. *Achillea tomentosa* (woolly yarrow) (4)
R. *Armeria maritima* (common thrift) (5)
S. *Geranium cinereum* (cranesbill) (6)
T. *Sedum spathulifolium* (stonecrop) (5)
U. *Geranium endressii* 'Wargrave Pink' (cranesbill) (4)
V. *Potentilla cinerea* (cinquefoil) (5)
W. *Dianthus plumarius* (cottage pink) (5)

Alternative Selections

A. *Cryptomeria japonica* 'Lobbii Nana' (Japanese cedar) (1)
C. *Jasminum parkeri* (dwarf jasmine) (2)
D. *Nandina domestica* 'Nana' (heavenly-bamboo) (2)
I. *Scaevola* × 'Mauve Clusters' (2)
V. *Bellis perennis* (English daisy) (5)

Geranium
endressii

Platycladus

Berberis

Geranium
cinereum

Helianthemum

Arabis

Rock Garden

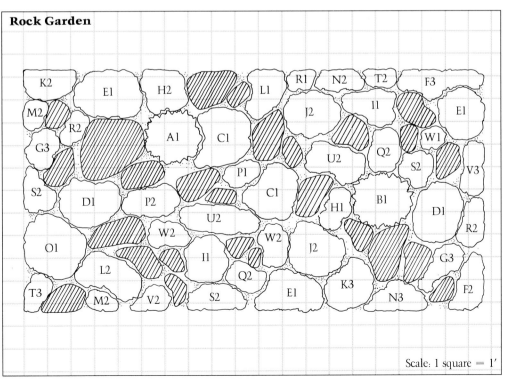

Scale: 1 square = 1'

Ferocactus

Artemisia

Sempervivum   Eriogonum   Opuntia

A DESERT GARDEN

Mention the word *desert* and the images that come to mind no doubt contain sand, rocks, cacti, and sagebrush. This desert garden offers those classic elements along with some southwestern standbys—yucca, agave, and an assortment of colorful wildflowers.

Aridity is only one desert characteristic. A desert that contains all the classic elements mentioned above will have fairly mild winter temperatures: Most cacti and succulents are unable to survive temperatures many degrees below freezing. Even though this desert planting scheme contains some of the most cold tolerant of those plants, it will succeed only in dry-summer parts of zones 8, 9, and 10. Gardeners in the dry-summer areas of zones 9 and 10 can choose from the alternative selections as

well. (In fact zone 10 gardeners can choose freely from any well-stocked cactus and succulent nursery.) The sagebrush in the main list may, in time, outgrow its space. If you don't want to bother with occasional restrictive pruning, choose the saltbush on the alternative list (though at the expense of the sagebrush aroma).

Naturally a desert garden needs full sun, and just as naturally it doesn't need frequent watering. Give these plants well-drained soil and apply water judiciously. Water all plants immediately after planting, then let the cacti establish new roots (a four- to eight-week process) before watering them again. The plants need water in spring, summer, and early fall; water thoroughly, then let the soil dry before watering again. In the dormant period, brought on by the shortening of days and cooler weather in fall and winter, water only if garden plants show signs of stress, such as shriveling or drooping.

A desert planting requires minimum maintenance, the occasional work focusing simply on neatness. In late winter, cut off spent stems from the evening primroses and California fuchsia; clear the garden of dead leaves and tidy up the plants. If necessary, prune the sagebrush or saltbush to control its size.

Variations

You can shorten this desert garden to 18 feet by drawing a line between the two points indicated on the plan, then planting only the larger portion. This leaves you with all the desert essence, except the tall fishhook barrel cactus.

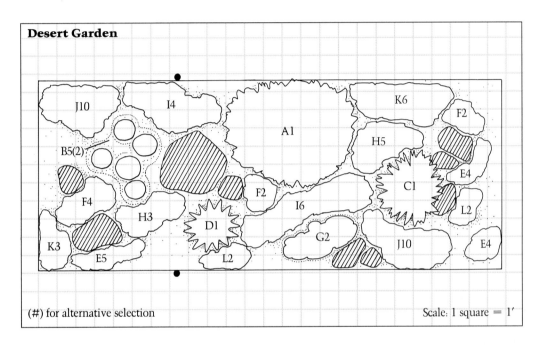

Desert Garden

(#) for alternative selection   Scale: 1 square = 1'

Opuntia basilaris
(beavertail cactus)

Desert-Garden Plants

A. *Artemisia tridentata* (big sagebrush) (1)
B. *Ferocactus wislizenii* (fishhook barrel cactus) (5)
C. *Yucca glauca* (small soapweed) (1)
D. *Agave utahensis* (Utah agave) (1)
E. *Sempervivum tectorum* (hen-and-chickens) (13)
F. *Pennisetum setaceum* 'Cupreum' (fountaingrass) (8)
G. *Opuntia basilaris* (beavertail) (2)
H. *Oenothera berlandieri* (Mexican evening primrose) (8)
I. *Oenothera stubbei* (*O. drummondii*) (Baja evening primrose) (10)
J. *Delosperma cooperi* (ice plant) (20)
K. *Zauschneria californica* var. *latifolia* (*Z. septentrionalis*) (California fuchsia) (9)
L. *Eriogonum umbellatum* (sulfurflower) (4)

Alternative Selections

A. *Atriplex canescens* (fourwing saltbush) (1)
B. *Lemaireocereus thurberi* (organpipe cactus) (2)
C. *Yucca harrimaniae* (1)
E. *Echeveria* × *imbricata* (hen-and-chicks) (13)
G. *Echinocereus engelmannii* (hedgehog cactus) (2)

AN APOTHECARY GARDEN

During the so-called Dark Ages in western Europe, the preservation and spread of knowledge was the province of the church. Included in this knowledge was the practice of medicine, and no respectable monastery would be without its apothecary garden of plants administered as remedies or preventives.

This planting scheme offers an attractive assortment of medieval medicinal plants. For easy access, a path separates the planting into two beds, which face a central sundial—to remind the attending monk both of the time of day and of the eternalness of time itself. Note the number of plants that bear the epithet *officinalis*, a Latin word ("of the shops") later applied to the plants that were standard components of medieval pharmacies.

All the plants on the main list will thrive in zones 5 through 9 and dry-summer zone 10. The alternative selections offer foliage variations for the same zones. By choosing any or all of the alternative plants, you can vary the color schemes in the garden.

Late winter or early spring is the time to clean out the previous year's dead foliage and spent stems and to prune the shrubs. Lightly head back the rose stems if the plant has become rangy. Cut back the southernwood to within a few inches of the ground, and cut back the English lavender by about half. Head back rue and garden sage as needed to keep these plants compact. In time, some of the perennials will start to spread beyond their allotted spaces. When this happens, simply remove a few plants. If a perennial becomes sparse or patchy, dig it up and divide and replant it in late winter or early spring. When the iris becomes crowded (in four or five years), dig it up and divide it in summer. Although the planting contains drought-tolerant plants and also two mints that are rampant in moist soil, routine garden watering suits them all. Place the beds where they'll receive sun for more than half the day.

Variations

By planting either one of the two beds, you will have a varied garden of apothecary plants that fits into a smaller space. To finish off either bed as a complete rectangle, plant pot marigolds in the semicircular inset along the front edge and include the sundial if you wish.

Foeniculum vulgare (common fennel)

Apothecary-Garden Plants

A. *Rosa gallica* 'Officinalis' ('Apothecary's Rose') (double French rose) (1)
B. *Ruta graveolens* (rue) (3)
C. *Valeriana officinalis* (valerian) (6)
D. *Lavandula angustifolia* (English lavender) (4)
E. *Foeniculum vulgare* (common fennel) (3)
F. *Levisticum officinale* (lovage) (1)
G. *Salvia officinalis* (garden sage) (4)
H. *Artemisia abrotanum* (southernwood) (2)
I. *Iris* × *germanica* var. *florentina* (orris) (6)
J. *Viola odorata* (sweet violet) (7)
K. *Marrubium vulgare* (horehound) (5)
L. *Melissa officinalis* (lemon balm) (4)
M. *Chrysanthemum balsamita* (costmary) (6)
N. *Symphytum officinale* (comfrey) (2)
O. *Origanum majorana* (sweet marjoram) (4)
P. *Thymus vulgaris* (common thyme) (7)
Q. *Stachys officinalis* (betony) (6)
R. *Mentha spicata* (spearmint) (2)
S. *Mentha* × *piperita* (peppermint) (4)
T. *Calendula officinalis* (pot marigold) (8)

Alternative Selections

B. *Ruta graveolens* 'Variegata' (variegated rue) (3)
E. *Foeniculum vulgare purpureum* (bronze fennel) (3)
G. *Salvia officinalis* 'Tricolor' (tricolor garden sage), *S. officinalis* 'Icterina' (variegated garden sage), or *S. officinalis* 'Purpurascens' (purpleleaf garden sage) (4)
L. *Melissa officinalis* 'Aurea' (variegated lemon balm) (4)
P. *Thymus vulgaris* 'Argenteus' (silver thyme) (7)
T. *Calendula officinalis*, a yellow or cream selection (pot marigold) (8)

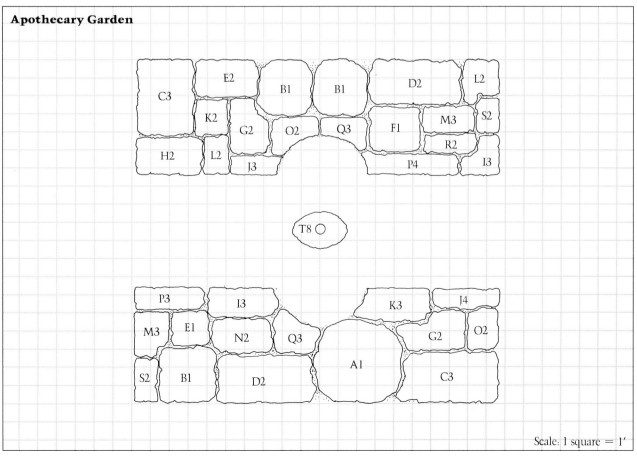

Apothecary Garden

Scale: 1 square = 1'

A DEVOTIONAL GARDEN

Although the Bible mentions numerous plants, many of them need the relatively mild winter of the holy land in order to survive—and today quite a few would be looked upon as weeds. To create an attractive planting with religious associations that will grow in zones 5 through 10, it was necessary to turn to the colder climate of western Europe and draw upon a variety of medieval devotional sources. Plants for this garden were gleaned from the great number of fifteenth-century artworks, tapestries, poems, carols and hymns, religious texts, and seasonal rituals associated with the Virgin Mary and the Christ Child. The alternative selections are additional choices for the same zones. The planting scheme was designed to accommodate a Madonna and Child statue.

Establish this bed where it will receive sun for more than half the day; give the plants routine garden watering. In late winter or early spring, clean out the dead leaves and spent flowering stems from the previous year's growth. To keep the roses shapely, lightly head

Alcea rosea (hollyhock)

Rosa

Alcea

Hesperis

Papaver

Alchemilla

Dianthus

Viola

Devotional-Garden Plants

A. *Rosa* × *alba* 'Semiplena' ('Alba semi-plena') (1)
B. *Rosa gallica* 'Officinalis' ('Apothecary's Rose') (double French rose) (1)
C. *Alchemilla mollis* (lady's-mantle) (10)
D. *Convallaria majalis* (lily-of-the-valley) (4)
E. *Dianthus caryophyllus* (carnation) (4)
F. *Iris* × *germanica* (flag) (2)
G. *Aquilegia vulgaris* (European columbine) (4)
H. *Lychnis coronaria* (crown-pink) (5)
I. *Lilium candidum* (Madonna lily) (5)
J. *Alcea rosea* (hollyhock) (6)
K. *Bellis perennis* (English daisy) (4)
L. *Viola odorata* (sweet violet) (10)
M. *Hesperis matronalis* (dames' rocket) (6)
N. *Calendula officinalis* (pot marigold) (9)
O. *Centaurea cyanus* (cornflower) (7)
P. *Papaver rhoeas* 'Flanders Field' (corn poppy) (8)

Alternative Selections

D. *Mentha spicata* (spearmint) (3)
K. *Viola tricolor* (herb-trinity, johnny-jump-up) (4)
L. *Vinca minor* (dwarf periwinkle) (6)

Alchemilla mollis (lady's-mantle)

them back if they need it. Replant the three annuals—pot marigold, cornflower, and corn poppy. If you choose the johnny-jump-up instead of the English daisy, set out new plants—or transplant the self-sown seedlings—each year. Every other year replace the biennial dames' rocket and hollyhock.

Variations

To make a shorter bed, with the statue at the center of the front edge, move the curved edge back to the two points indicated on the plan. You will lose one planting of lady's-mantle and all of the English daisy, cornflower, and pot marigold.

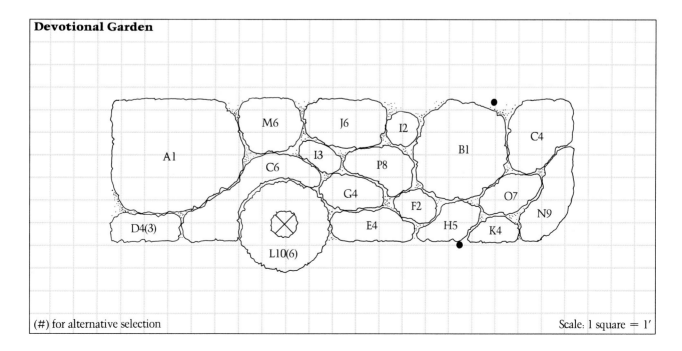

Devotional Garden

M6　J6　I2　C4
A1　I3　B1
C6　P8
G4　O7
F2
D4(3)　E4　H5　K4　N9
L10(6)

(#) for alternative selection　　　Scale: 1 square = 1′

A SHAKESPEARE GARDEN

From Titania's bower in *A Midsummer Night's Dream* to Perdita's rustic garden in *The Winter's Tale*, Shakespeare's writings abound with references to plants and gardens. What a simple pleasure, then, to establish a quiet garden enclave with plants that recall the bard.

Most of Shakespeare's plants that we would consider garden worthy won't survive winters in zones 3, 4, and 5; quite a few can't take even the low temperatures in zone 6. The planting suggested here contains some of the most adaptable of his plants, suitable for many zones. All the plants on the main list will grow in zones 6 through 9, although the potted laurel will need to be taken indoors during the winter in zones 6, 7, and 8. Gardeners in zone 9 and dry-summer zone 10 will want to choose the Japanese boxwood instead of the common box-

wood, and one of the alternative dwarf apple selections, and may prefer the alternate for the potted laurel. The alternative English daisy and iris will succeed in zones 6 through 10. Place these beds where they'll receive sun for at least six hours a day.

The year's maintenance starts with cleanup and pruning—either in fall, or in late winter or early spring before growth begins. Clear out the dead leaves and flowering stems of the perennials, and remove the spent annuals—larkspur and pot marigold. In late winter or early spring, remove the unproductive wood from the roses and head back any wayward canes to shape the plants (though remember that pruning these roses before they bloom sacrifices some of the spring flowers). Also head back halfway the English lavender, common wormwood, and hyssop; and head back the rue stems as needed to keep them shapely. Set out new plants of larkspur and pot marigold. During the growing season, shear the boxwood and English lavender hedges as often as needed to suit your sense of neatness. Give the plants routine garden watering.

Variations

This scheme was designed as a cozy nook in a corner of the garden, where you might sit and read among "literary" plants. Either bed, though, could stand on its own as an individual planting.

Shakespeare-Garden Plants

A. *Rosa gallica* 'Versicolor' ('Rosa Mundi') (3)
B. *Malus pumila* on dwarfing rootstock (apple) (1)
C. *Rosa eglanteria* (eglantine, sweetbrier) (1)
D. *Rosa × alba* 'Semiplena' ('Alba semi-plena') (1)
E. *Rosa × alba* 'Incarnata' ('Great Maidens Blush') (1)
F. *Ruta graveolens* (rue) (1)
G. *Artemisia absinthium* (common wormwood) (2)
H. *Buxus sempervirens* (common boxwood) (40, 17 or more)
I. *Lavandula angustifolia* (English lavender) (11)
J. *Rheum rhabarbarum* (rhubarb) (2)
K. *Lilium candidum* (Madonna lily) (3)
L. *Hyssopus officinalis* (hyssop) (3)
M. *Aquilegia vulgaris* (European columbine) (4)
N. *Dianthus plumarius* (cottage pink) (7)
O. *Chamaemelum nobile* (chamomile) (9)
P. *Consolida ambigua* (larkspur) (8)
Q. *Calendula officinalis* (pot marigold) (6)
R. *Laurus nobilis*, in pot (laurel) (1)
S. *Thymus vulgaris* (common thyme) (1)
T. *Viola odorata* (sweet violet) (18)

Alternative Selections

B. *Malus pumila* 'Beverly Hills', 'Ein Shemer', or 'Gordon' on dwarfing rootstock (apple) (1)
H. *Buxus microphylla* var. *japonica* (Japanese boxwood) (40, 17 or more)
J. *Bellis perennis* (English daisy) (16)
K. *Iris pseudacorus* (yellow flag) (1)
R. *Citrus limon* (lemon) or *C. sinensis* (orange), in pot (1)

Buxus sempervirens (common boxwood)

Malus

Rosa

Lavandula

Buxus

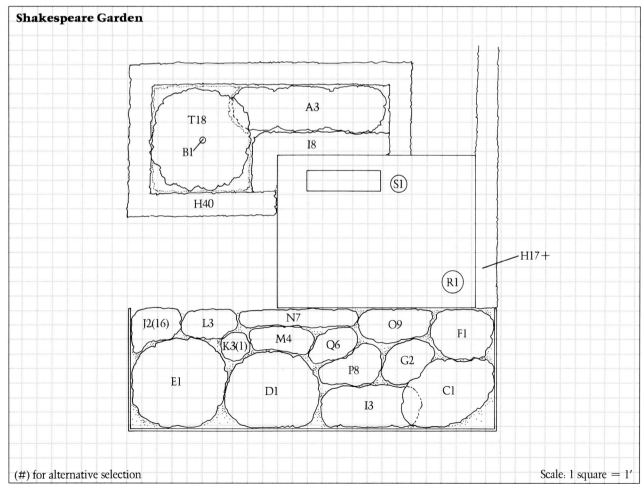

Shakespeare Garden

T18

B1

A3

I8

H40

S1

H17+

R1

J2(16) L3 N7 O9 F1

K3(1) M4 Q6 G2

E1 D1 P8 C1

I3

(#) for alternative selection

Scale: 1 square = 1'

Ruta

Foeniculum

Lavandula

AN HERB GARDEN

The traditional herb garden is a romantic notion perhaps no more than one hundred years
old. In it are combined curative plants of the
medieval apothecary gardens, culinary herbs
from the kitchen garden, and diverse other
plants that simply assort well with these. The
traditional style of herb garden, fully realized
in Edwardian times, emphasized the aesthetic
relationship between the plants and favored
those that were pleasantly aromatic so that the
garden would be pleasing to eyes and nose
alike. Some of these gardens were formal in
design, recalling knot gardens and European
parterres; others were more in tune with the
cottage garden style, their artfully haphazard
arrangements bordered by an herbal hedge.

This herb garden incorporates both a cottage effect and a little formality, and offers an
enchanting cross section of herbs of all sorts.
The sundial is in the Edwardian style; the
bench—a timeless garden amenity—is a place
to pause and absorb the romance of it all. Although several plants boast a striking flower
display (especially the English lavender,
beebalm, and common yarrow), much of the
beauty of this garden lies in the relationships
between foliage of differing colors and textures. All the plants but three will thrive in
zones 6 through 9 and dry-summer zone 10. The
potted rosemary and geranium will need to be
brought indoors during winter in zones 6 and 7.
In zone 10, instead of beebalm choose the alternative selection, golden feverfew. The other alternative selections are presented as options to
vary the planting. Give the plants full sun and
moderate to routine watering. Well-drained soil
is preferable—and in summer-rainfall regions
it is a requirement.

Trimming and tidying are your maintenance obligations to this herb planting. In fall,
late winter, or early spring, remove the dead
leaves and cut out last year's flowering stems
on the common yarrow, costmary, beebalm,
and lamb's-ears. Then in late winter or early
spring, cut back by half the English lavender,
the garden sages, hyssop, and oregano. This is
also an appropriate time to even up the germander border. Later in the year you may need
to lightly clip it again to keep it neat. The
bronze fennel may seed prolifically in zones 7
through 10, so in those zones it is better to cut
it back toward the end of the growing season
(late summer or early fall) before its seeds
ripen and scatter. Trim as needed, not always
every year, the silver thyme, common wormwood, southernwood, lavender-cotton, and rue
to keep them from becoming rangy or sparse.

Chrysanthemum

Artemisia

Teucrium

Tanacetum vulgare
(common tansy)

To ensure winter survival in zone 6, protect the English lavender, lavender-cotton, and winter savory with evergreen boughs or a loose covering of salt hay in late fall.

Variations

Although designed as a peaceful enclave, this planting can be reduced to two L-shaped plans, either of which can be slotted into a smaller space. To make the smaller of the two L shapes, draw a line from the back of the bed to the front, separating the English lavender from the fennel, hyssop, and thyme; plant the portion with the lavender, eliminate the bench, and continue the germander border in front of the English lavender, wrapping it around to the back. For a larger bed, draw a line on the other side of the English lavender from the back of the bed to the front and plant the portion containing the lavender. In this option, retain the bench and wrap a germander border around the end of the English lavender.

Herb Garden

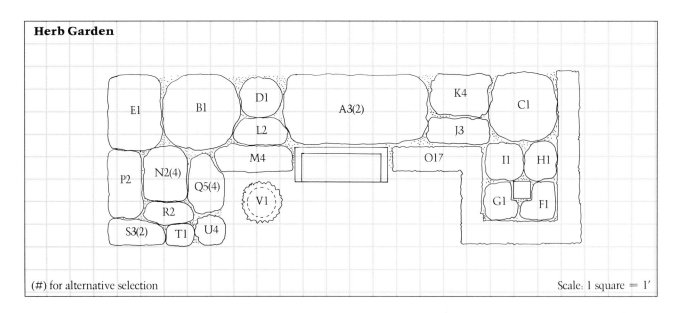

(#) for alternative selection   Scale: 1 square = 1'

Herb-Garden Plants

A. *Lavandula angustifolia* (English lavender) (3)
B. *Ruta graveolens* (rue) (1)
C. *Artemisia absinthium* (common wormwood) (1)
D. *Foeniculum vulgare purpureum* (bronze fennel) (1)
E. *Artemisia abrotanum* (southernwood) (1)
F. *Salvia officinalis* (garden sage) (1)
G. *Salvia officinalis* 'Icterina' (variegated garden sage) (1)
H. *Salvia officinalis* 'Tricolor' (tricolor garden sage) (1)
I. *Salvia officinalis* 'Purpurascens' (purpleleaf garden sage) (1)
J. *Achillea millefolium* (common yarrow) (3)
K. *Chrysanthemum balsamita* (costmary) (4)
L. *Hyssopus officinalis* (hyssop) (2)
M. *Thymus vulgaris* 'Argenteus' (silver thyme) (4)
N. *Monarda didyma* (beebalm) (2)
O. *Teucrium chamaedrys* (germander) (17)
P. *Santolina chamaecyparissus* (lavender-cotton) (2)
Q. *Chamaemelum nobile* (chamomile) (5)
R. *Origanum vulgare* (oregano) (2)
S. *Stachys byzantina* (lamb's-ears) (3)
T. *Satureja montana* (winter savory) (1)
U. *Allium schoenoprasum* (chives) (4)
V. *Rosmarinus officinalis*, in pot (rosemary) (1)

Alternative Selections

A. *Rosa gallica* 'Officinalis' ('Apothecary's Rose') (2)
D. *Tanacetum vulgare* (common tansy) (1)
K. *Marrubium vulgare* (horehound) (4)
N. *Chrysanthemum parthenium* 'Aureum' (golden feverfew) (4)
Q. *Melissa officinalis* (lemon balm) (4)
S. *Nepeta cataria* (catnip) (2)
T. *Rumex scutatus* (French sorrel) (1)
V. *Pelargonium odoratissimum* (apple geranium) (1)

Achillea millefolium (common yarrow)

Origanum vulgare (oregano)

A FRAGRANT GARDEN

Fragrance is the intangible attribute that places many attractive flowers into the "especially beautiful" category. And it also elevates a number of more mundane plants to a "special" status. A pleasing aroma not only enhances the moment, it also calls up fond memories indelibly associated with the particular scent. What, then, could be more soul-satisfying than a corner of your garden devoted to olfactory as well as visual pleasure?

Flower and plant aromas are almost infinitely varied, and the dispersal of the scents takes several forms. Some blossoms release their fragrance into the air, perfuming a garden from a distance. Others reveal their scented treasure only when you put your nose into their petals. And the aromatic-foliage plants may not disclose their essential oils until you brush against or bruise their leaves. This garden contains representatives of all three types of fragrant plants.

From the first violets in late winter or early spring to the final roses of fall, this fragrance planting will offer flowers and scent almost continually. The peak display will be in early to mid-summer, when all but the violets, iris, and peony will be blooming. Give the plants at least six hours of sun each day and routine garden watering. With two exceptions, the plants in the main list will grow in zones 5 through 9 and dry-summer zone 10. The apple geranium (in the container) will have to spend winter where it is protected from frost in zones 5 through 9; and the peony's need for winter chilling spoils the quality of its performance in zones 9 and 10. The alternative list gives a peony substitute—the wallflower—for zones 9 and 10, as well as several notably fragrant options for those two warm zones.

In zones 5 and 6, the Penelope rose should receive winter protection in mid- to late fall; see Ortho's book *All About Roses* for recommended methods of protecting roses. In all zones, yearly maintenance starts in late winter or early spring with cleanup and pruning. Clear out dead leaves, spent flower stems, and remains of last year's annuals: flowering tobacco, mignonette, and sweet alyssum. Remove winter protection from the Penelope rose if necessary, then prune all the roses just to shape them. Cut back halfway the English lavender and southernwood, and cut back the butterfly bush to 6 to 12 inches from the ground. Replant the sweet alyssum and mignonette when you can work the soil; set out new flowering tobacco plants when the soil has warmed. Replace plantings of cheddar pink, cottage pink, and

Fragrant Garden

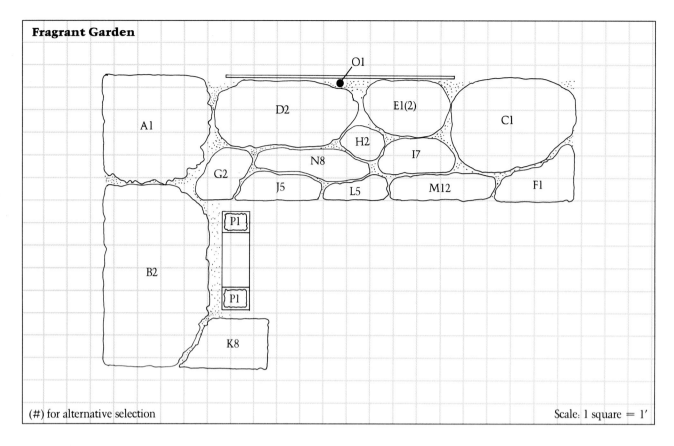

O1

D2

E1(2)

C1

A1

H2

I7

N8

G2

J5   L5   M12   F1

P1

B2

P1

K8

(#) for alternative selection   Scale: 1 square = 1'

Fragrant-Garden Plants

A. *Buddleia davidii* (common butterfly bush) (1)
B. *Rosa* 'Penelope' (2)
C. *Rosa* 'Frau Dagmar Hartopp' (1)
D. *Lavandula angustifolia* (English lavender) (2)
E. *Paeonia lactiflora* 'Mons. Jules Elie' (peony) (1)
F. *Artemisia abrotanum* (southernwood) (1)
G. *Iris*, tall bearded hybrid 'Victoria Falls' (2)
H. *Lilium candidum* (Madonna lily) (2)
I. *Dianthus plumarius* (cottage pink) (7)
J. *Dianthus gratianopolitanus* (cheddar pink) (5)
K. *Viola odorata* (sweet violet) (8)
L. *Reseda odorata* (mignonette) (5)
M. *Lobularia maritima* (sweet alyssum) (12)
N. *Nicotiana alata* (flowering tobacco) (8)
O. *Lonicera periclymenum* 'Serotina' (woodbine) (1)
P. *Pelargonium odoratissimum*, in container (apple geranium) (2)

Alternative Selections

A. *Osmanthus fragrans* (sweet olive) (1)
E. *Erysimum linifolium* 'Variegatum' (*Cheiranthus linifolius*) (wallflower) (2)
O. *Trachelospermum jasminoides* (starjasmine) (1)
P. *Gardenia jasminoides* 'Veitchii', in container (gardenia) (2)

wallflower with cuttings or new plants when existing plantings become sparse and rangy. Dig and divide the bearded iris every third or fourth summer.

Variations

You can alter the shape of this planting (though you'll sacrifice a place to rest and savor the scents) by extending the longest line so that it separates the butterfly bush from the Penelope roses, then planting just the long rectangle. If you want to retain the L shape and bench in a shorter plan, you can eliminate the southernwood, the Frau Dagmar Hartopp rose, and about one third of the sweet alyssum.

Nicotiana alata (flowering tobacco)

A MEDITERRANEAN GARDEN

Blue skies, sunshine, and warmth: These are usually the first qualities evoked by mention of the word *Mediterranean*. Native plants of the region also contribute to the Mediterranean essence. The foliage often is gray or dull green rather than bright green; many plants have flowers of yellow, blue, or white, mirroring sunshine, blue skies, and summer clouds of the Mediterranean region. And aroma plays a large part: the honeyed scent of broom, the grapelike fragrance of iris, the unique spicy odor of rockrose foliage, and the special fragrance that made lavender famous.

The Mediterranean climate features warm, dry summers and moist, fairly mild winters. In dry-summer regions, this garden will prosper in zones 8, 9, and 10. In regions where summer combines high temperatures and humidity, the planting will succeed in zone 8 and the cooler parts of zone 9. By choosing plants from the alternative selections, gardeners in zone 7 also can enjoy a fragment of Mediterranean landscape. In all regions, establish the planting in full sun.

Except for the chaste tree and smoke tree, all the plants retain their foliage throughout the year. And with the mixture of gray and differing green leaves, the garden planting

Acanthus mollis
(bear's-breech)

will be attractive at all times. Floral interest begins in late winter or early spring with the chartreuse-flowered euphorbia, then picks up tempo for a peak display in mid- to late spring. In summer, the chaste tree and smoke tree set the tone with cool blue flowers and bronzy purple foliage, respectively, while the anthemis spreads carpets of yellow-centered white daisies, which contrast with the blue of the ground morning glory.

This Mediterranean garden qualifies both as a low-maintenance and a low-water-use area. In fact, where regular watering is unavoidable (as in summer-rainfall regions) be very sure to

Vitex

Teucrium

Cotinus

Achillea

Helianthemum

Cytisus

Lychnis

Santolina

Iris

Cistus

Helianthemum

Mediterranean Garden

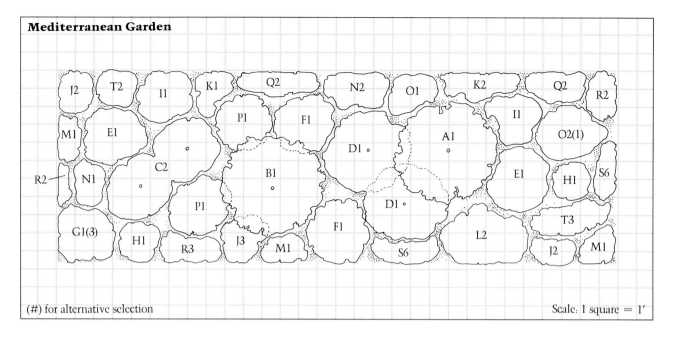

(#) for alternative selection   Scale: 1 square = 1'

establish the planting in soil that drains well. Tidy gardeners may want to remove the spent flowering stems of the perennials—iris, euphorbia, bear's-breech, crown-pink, yarrow, and lamb's-ears—as the flowers fade. If you let the euphorbia, crown-pink, and lamb's-ears set seed, you will get many volunteer seedlings. The bulk of the annual maintenance comes in late winter or early spring, when you should clean out any conspicuous dead leaves and last year's flowering stems, if you haven't already done so. Before the flush of new growth, head back the shrubs and spreading perennials as needed to prevent them from becoming rangy. The crown-pink may need replacing every two years; divide and replant the iris and lamb's-ears about every three or four years.

Variations

The floral color scheme mixes white, yellow tones, and shades of blue, including lavender and violet. To inject a dash of pink, you could replace the white rockrose with *Cistus* 'Doris Hiberson' (clear pink), *Cistus incanus* (lilac pink), or *Cistus* 'Sunset' (dark purplish pink). For a shorter rectangular bed, divide the planting down the middle and take either the left or right half (so that you have either the smoke tree or the chaste tree). Then add 2 feet to the length and plant the edge with your choice of low plants: lamb's-ears, sun-rose, yarrow, ground morning glory, anthemis, or germander. For a somewhat narrower bed to go against a wall or fence, eliminate the back row of plants.

To lengthen the planting, spread from the center, using perhaps two chaste trees and two smoke trees and filling in with additional plants of bush germander, Provence bloom, and artemisia.

Mediterranean-Garden Plants

A. *Cotinus coggygria* 'Purpureus' (purple smoke tree) (1)
B. *Vitex agnus-castus* (chaste tree) (1)
C. *Phlomis fruticosa* (Jerusalem sage) (2)
D. *Teucrium fruticans* (bush germander) (2)
E. *Cistus* × *hybridus* (white rockrose) (2)
F. *Cytisus purgans* (Provence broom) (2)
G. *Cistus salviifolius* (sageleaf rockrose) (1)
H. *Euphorbia characias wulfenii* (euphorbia) (2)
I. *Acanthus mollis* (bear's-breech) (2)
J. *Iris* 'Pallida Variegata' (iris) (7)
K. *Teucrium chamaedrys* (germander) (3)
L. *Santolina virens* (green santolina) (2)
M. *Helianthemum nummularium*, any color (sun-rose) (3)
N. *Lavandula angustifolia* 'Hidcote' (English lavender) (3)
O. *Anthemis cupaniana* (anthemis) (3)
P. *Artemisia* × 'Powis Castle' (2)
Q. *Convolvulus mauritanicus* (ground morning glory) (4)
R. *Stachys byzantina* (lamb's-ears) (7)
S. *Lychnis coronaria* (crown-pink) (12)
T. *Achillea taygetea* (yarrow) (5)

Alternative Selections

E. *Ruta graveolens* (rue) (2)
G. *Iberis sempervirens* (evergreen candytuft) (3)
O. *Santolina chamaecyparissus* (lavender-cotton) (2)

A BIRD GARDEN

Birds will be drawn to the garden that has hotel accommodations—food, drink, and places to spend the night. Berries, seeds, and insects in the broad sense constitute food; water is the drink. Shelter can be a variety of plants allowed to grow together in an unmanicured fashion that mimics the natural landscape. Important to the design of a bird planting is the edging effect that you see in a forest clearing, where shrubs of various heights bridge the transition from tree to grassland.

This plan for a bird corner includes a little of everything that a wide variety of birds find appealing. Berry-eating birds will gravitate to the serviceberry, Washington thorn, rose, euonymus, dogwoods, honeysuckle, and—late in the season—the cotoneaster, barberry, and bearberry. (In zones 7 through 10, the firethorn produces irresistible berries.) Seedeaters will flock to the sunflowers, goldenrod, and Chinese pennisetum (or alternative fountaingrass),

while those that favor insects will seek out the fine eating on the Washington thorn, the rose, and the firethorn in particular. Even hummingbirds will be tempted into the garden, drawn by the blossoms of the honeysuckle and coralbells. The birdbath will be a universal lure for bathing and drinking; a pathway of gravel or plain earth will encourage dustbaths. And the intertwining shrub growth, some of it thorny, will provide safe bird nesting sites.

Although this planting is aimed at satisfying the specific needs of birds, you'll find it is visually attractive as well, with colorful flowers or fruits appearing at all times of year. Several shrubs also will display impressive autumn foliage color before shedding their leaves for the year. The main planting list is suitable in zones 5, 6, and 7, where winter cold rules out most evergreen trees and shrubs other than conifers. Gardeners in zone 8 may use the main list or any of the plants given in the alternative

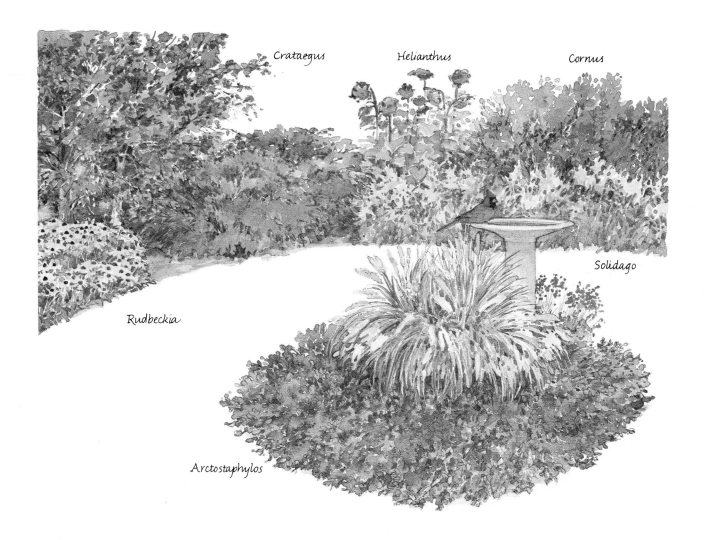

selections list. In zone 9 and dry-summer zone 10, where winter temperatures are mild, be sure to use the alternative selections.

Because birds are attracted to naturalistic plantings, yearly maintenance is minimal. Let leaf-litter accumulate as much as your sense of neatness will allow: Birds will forage in it for insects and seeds. In late winter or early spring, cut last year's spent stems of black-eyed-susan, goldenrod, and Chinese pennisetum or fountaingrass. If the seeds haven't already been dispersed or eaten by the birds, shake them out on the ground. When the soil warms, set out new sunflower plants. Prune shrubs only as needed to correct wayward or unbalanced growth.

Variations

The larger the planting, the more inviting it is to birds. However, you can reduce the size of the garden and still present an alluring assortment of plants. Draw a line between the Siberian dogwood and sunflower, and plant only the part that contains the Siberian dogwood. For a less abrupt edge, add 3 feet to the planting and wrap the goldenrod (adding five more plants) around the end of the dogwood.

Berberis thunbergii 'Atropurpurea' (redleaf Japanese barberry)

Bird-Garden Plants

A. *Crataegus phaenopyrum* (Washington thorn) (2)
B. *Amelanchier* × *grandiflora* (apple serviceberry) (1)
C. *Picea pungens* 'Fat Albert' (Colorado spruce) (1)
D. *Rosa* 'Ballerina' (2)
E. *Euonymus alata* 'Compacta' (winged euonymus) (2)
F. *Cornus alba* 'Sibirica' (Siberian dogwood) (2)
G. *Cotoneaster horizontalis* (rock cotoneaster) (2)
H. *Berberis thunbergii* (Japanese barberry) (3)
I. *Lonicera tatarica* (Tatarian honeysuckle) (1)
J. *Rudbeckia hirta* 'Marmalade' (black-eyed-susan) (26)
K. *Cornus sericea* (*C. stolonifera*) 'Kelseyi' (redtwig dogwood) (8)
L. *Solidago* × 'Cloth of Gold' (goldenrod) (10)
M. *Helianthus annuus* (common sunflower) (9)
N. *Pennisetum alopecuroides* (Chinese pennisetum) (5)
O. *Heuchera sanguinea* (coralbells) (8)
P. *Arctostaphylos uva-ursi* (bearberry) (6)

Alternative Selections

B. *Prunus* × *cistena* (dwarf redleaf plum) (1)
C. *Pyracantha coccinea* (firethorn) (1)
E. *Viburnum opulus* 'Compactum' (European cranberry bush) (2)
F. *Ligustrum japonicum* 'Texanum' (Japanese privet) (2)
H. *Ilex cornuta* 'Berries Jubilee' (Chinese holly) (3)
K. *Mahonia aquifolium* 'Compacta' (Oregon grape) (8)
N. *Pennisetum setaceum* (fountaingrass) (5)

Left: *Ligustrum japonicum* 'Texanum' (Japanese privet)
Right: *Lonicera tatarica* (Tatarian honeysuckle)

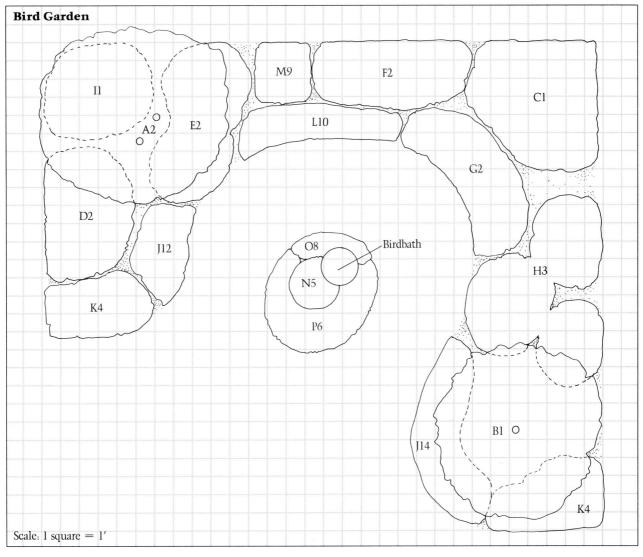

Bird Garden

I1

A2

E2

M9

F2

C1

L10

G2

D2

J12

O8

N5

P6

Birdbath

H3

K4

J14

B1

K4

Scale: 1 square = 1′

Buddleia   Lonicera   Kniphofia   Weigela

Heuchera

A HUMMINGBIRD GARDEN

Hummingbirds possess a universal charm. Their iridescent plumage immediately attracts attention, and their unique method of flight and overall panache inspire wonder and admiration. A staple of the hummingbird's diet is flower nectar—nature's sugar solution—which supplies energy for their incessant motion. A sure way to attract hummingbirds, then, is to offer an abundance of their favorite nectar-bearing flowers, ideally in a windless part of your garden.

Brightly colored flowers are a powerful hummingbird attractant. Red and orange shades seem to be the most popular colors, though blue and pink also come in for their share of attention. Funnel-shaped and tubular blossoms also pique their curiosity, offering the hope of nectar at the base of the flowers.

The plants in this hummingbird garden, therefore, focus on the red sector of the spectrum, from the orange butterfly weed to the red-purple butterfly bush, and including the warm pink shades of summer phlox, coralbells, and foxglove. Flowering starts in spring with coralbells, scarlet trumpet or gold flame honeysuckle, and foxglove; reaches a peak in summer; then fades in fall with the last blooms of scarlet sage, petunia, flowering tobacco, and beardtongue.

Hummingbirds in variety frequent gardens in the West and Southwest; east of the plains, only one—the Ruby-throated Hummingbird—visits during the year's warmer months. The main plant list covers eastern and western gardens in zones 5 through 9; plants in the alternative list can be used in western zone 9 gardens and should be used in dry-summer zone 10.

Hummingbird-Garden Plants

A. *Lonicera × brownii* 'Dropmore Scarlet' (scarlet trumpet honeysuckle) (1)
B. *Weigela* 'Bristol Ruby' (weigela) (1)
C. *Buddleia davidii* 'Nanho Purple' (common butterfly bush) (1)
D. *Asclepias tuberosa* (butterfly weed) (1)
E. *Penstemon barbatus* 'Prairie Fire' (beardtongue) (13)
F. *Heuchera sanguinea* (coralbells) (17)
G. *Kniphofia uvaria* (red-hot-poker) (3)
H. *Digitalis × mertonensis* (foxglove) (7)
I. *Monarda didyma* 'Cambridge Scarlet' (beebalm) (3)
J. *Nicotiana alata*, red or pink selection (flowering tobacco) (14)
K. *Petunia × hybrida*, red selection (petunia) (16)
L. *Phlox paniculata*, orange or red cultivar, such as 'Orange Perfection' (summer phlox) (4)
M. *Salvia splendens* (scarlet sage) (10)

Alternative Selections

A. *Lonicera heckrottii* (gold flame honeysuckle) (1)
B. *Buddleia davidii* (common butterfly bush) (1)
C. *Salvia greggii* (autumn sage) (1)
E. *Aquilegia*, long-spurred hybrid (columbine) (13)
I. *Mimulus cardinalis* (scarlet monkeyflower) (1)
L. *Penstemon × gloxinioides* (border penstemon) (6)

As soon as the weather permits gardening in late winter or early spring, clean up the planting, removing dead leaves and the spent plants of last year's annuals: flowering tobacco, petunias, and scarlet sage. Cut back the old flowering stems of the perennials—beardtongue, foxglove, summer phlox, and beebalm. Prune the butterfly bush to 6 to 12 inches from the ground. Thin and train the scarlet trumpet or gold flame honeysuckle as needed. Head back any wayward growth on the weigela, but wait until after it has flowered to prune it for size. When the soil warms, set out new plants of the annuals.

Variations

The recommended plants play to the hummingbird's favorite color: red. If this scheme is too vibrant for your taste, you can alter it by choosing alternative colors for various plants. Use a pink-flowered beardtongue, such as Rose Elf; a pink-flowered beebalm, such as Croftway Pink; a white-flowering tobacco; pink, blue, or purple selections of petunia; pink or lavender cultivars of summer phlox; or violet-flowered scarlet sage.

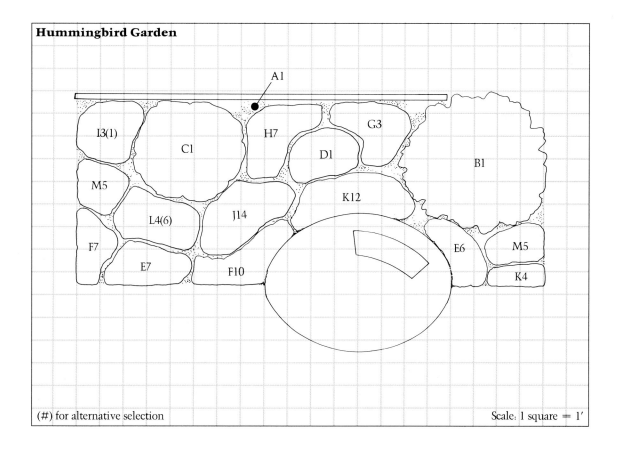

Hummingbird Garden

A1 · I3(1) · C1 · H7 · G3 · D1 · B1 · M5 · L4(6) · J14 · K12 · F7 · E7 · F10 · E6 · M5 · K4

(#) for alternative selection   Scale: 1 square = 1'

Buddleia

Eupatorium

Spiraea

Coreopsis lanceolata

Sedum

A BUTTERFLY GARDEN

Who can be unmoved by butterflies? Like fragile works of art, they lazily float in and out of our gardens on warm, sunny days, searching for food in nectar-laden blossoms. Although the particular butterflies vary from one part of the country to another, a sure way to lure them to your own garden, no matter where you live, is to plant their favorite flowers.

In this butterfly garden are assembled 13 noted butterfly attractants. The flowering starts in mid- to late spring with the catmint. In mid- to late summer, it peaks with the tall joe-pye-weed, common butterfly bush, and butterfly weed dominating the show. It then continues into fall until cool weather calls a halt.

Establish this bed in full sun—perhaps in a lawn—and give plants routine watering. Gardeners in zones 5 through 9 can use plants in the main list; dry-summer zone 10 gardeners should choose the alternative selections,

replacing the joe-pye-weed with lantana and the spiraea with white Jupiter's-beard.

A standard cleanup, in late winter or early spring, is the major maintenance for the year. Clear out dead leaves, dead plants of last year's flowering tobacco, and spent flowering stems on the perennials. Cut back the common butterfly bush to 6 to 12 inches from the ground, and cut back by about half the English lavender, spiraea, and catmint. Eventually, you will need to dig up most of the perennials in early spring and divide them to rejuvenate the plantings. First among these, after several years, will be the black-eyed-susan, both forms of coreopsis, and the common yarrow.

Variations

If you want a smaller, shallower bed, you can cut the planting in half by drawing a line connecting the dots in the margin. Plant whichever half appeals more to you.

Rudbeckia hirta (black-eyed-susan)

Butterfly-Garden Plants

A. *Buddleia davidii* (common butterfly bush) (1)
B. *Eupatorium maculatum* (joe-pye-weed) (2)
C. *Asclepias tuberosa* (butterfly weed) (3)
D. *Lavandula angustifolia* (English lavender) (4)
E. *Sedum spectabile* or *S. telephium* 'Autumn Joy' (stonecrop) (5)
F. *Achillea millefolium* (common yarrow) (9)
G. *Nepeta* × *faassenii* (catmint) (6)
H. *Spiraea* × *bumalda* 'Anthony Waterer' (spiraea) (3)
I. *Coreopsis lanceolata* (coreopsis) (3)
J. *Coreopsis verticillata* 'Moonbeam' (coreopsis) (5)
K. *Hemerocallis*, yellow-flowered cultivar (daylily) (6)
L. *Nicotiana alata* (flowering tobacco) (15)
M. *Rudbeckia hirta* 'Marmalade' (black-eyed-susan) (6)

Alternative Selections

B. *Lantana camara* (lantana) (2)
H. *Centranthus ruber* 'Albus' (white Jupiter's-beard) (7)

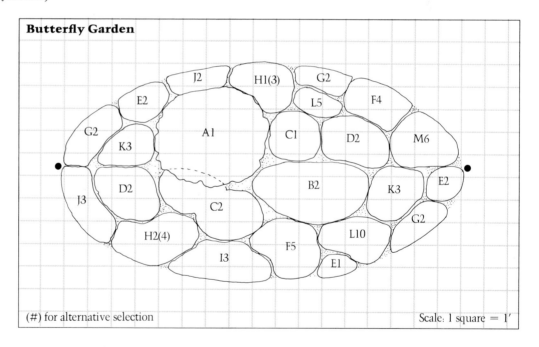

Butterfly Garden

(#) for alternative selection   Scale: 1 square = 1'

Left: *Nicotiana alata*
(flowering tobacco)
Right: *Lantana camara*
(lantana)

A MINIATURE GARDEN

One of the most compelling reasons for "gardening small" has always been limited space. Now, with the hastening pace of life and multiple demands on time, an increasingly important reason is fewer hours to devote to gardening. Small-garden planning, though, raises an immediate choice: quickly fill the space with a few normal-sized plants, or spend some time tracking down a greater number of naturally small plants to create a varied, scaled-down landscape. For the real gardening enthusiast, there's only one decision! This planting scheme presents an assortment of attractive, easy-to-grow plants in a miniature landscape that will provide interest throughout the growing season in a space only 12 feet long by 5 feet wide. Children interested in starting a garden may find this an especially rewarding project.

This garden was designed for full sun in zones 5 through 9 and dry-summer zone 10. Four of the five alternative selections are optional choices for gardeners in zones 9 and 10; the jade plant choice is for zone 10 only.

Because the plants, themselves, are small and feature smallish flowers and fine-textured foliage, this planting looks better in a bed raised above the soil grade. You could use railroad ties, construction timbers, or two or more courses of brick to make just a slight elevation that would show it off well. Plants should have well-drained, reasonably good garden soil and routine garden watering.

Just in advance of the growing season, in late winter or early spring, tidy up the planting. Remove the dead leaves and any spent stems of last year's flowers. Cut back the roses and evergreen candytuft by about half, and trim any plants that are encroaching on their neighbors. Head back any rangy stems on the pine to maintain compactness, cutting them back to branching stems or to the base of a year's growth. During the growing season, groom the planting to keep it neat. In zones 5, 6, and 7, apply a winter protection of evergreen boughs or salt hay in late fall or as soon as the soil freezes; this will offset the freeze-thaw cycles that can damage raised-bed plantings in the colder zones.

Pinus   Arabis   Rosa

Variations

This planting wasn't designed to be altered in size, but you can vary the color scheme by selecting different cultivars. Instead of the suggested white or pink roses, which assort well with the crimson Tiny Rubies dianthus, you could select a pink dianthus and a red miniature rose or choose a scarlet selection of maiden pink (*Dianthus deltoides*), which would contrast brightly with an orange or yellow rose.

Left: *Dianthus* (pink)

Sedum spathulifolium (stonecrop)

Miniature-Garden Plants

A. *Pinus mugo* var. *mugo* (mugo pine) (1)
B. *Rosa*, miniature hybrid, such as 'Popcorn' or 'Rosemarin' (5)
C. *Iberis sempervirens* 'Little Gem' (evergreen candytuft) (10)
D. *Campanula portenschlagiana* (Dalmatian bellflower) (3)
E. *Arabis caucasica* (wall rockcress) (3)
F. *Dianthus* 'Tiny Rubies' (pink) (7)
G. *Thymus pseudolanuginosus* (woolly thyme) (4)
H. *Festuca ovina* var. *glauca* (blue fescue) (5)
I. *Sedum spathulifolium* (stonecrop) (2)
J. *Anacyclus depressus* (anacyclus) (2)
K. *Sagina subulata* (Irish moss) (1 or 2 flats: 2-inch squares cut and planted 6 inches apart)

Alternative Selections

A. *Crassula argentea* 'Variegata' (variegated jade plant) (1)
D. *Campanula poscharskyana* (Serbian bellflower) (2)
E. *Erodium chamaedryoides* (alpine geranium) (3)
H. *Rhodohypoxis baurii* (rhodohypoxis) (10)
J. *Cotula squalida* (New Zealand brassbuttons) (2)

Miniature Garden

D3(2) E3
A1 F7 B5
Pool
C4 H3(6) G4 K
J2 H2(4) I2 C6

(#) for alternative selection   Scale: 1 square = 1′

Pinus mugo var. *mugo* (mugo pine)

A KITCHEN GARDEN

Like the apothecary garden (see pages 52 to 53), the kitchen garden traces its roots to medieval times and beyond, when communities had to be self-sufficient. While apothecary plants cared for bodily ailments, kitchen plants provided edibles of all sorts to nurture the body. Nowadays, the most common planting of edibles is the vegetable garden; this kitchen garden scheme returns to the older and more all-encompassing concept that includes not only vegetables but also culinary herbs and fruit crops. It also acknowledges the contemporary desire for fresh flowers in the home by including an assortment of productive annuals and a perennial for cutting.

The plants in the larger bed are those that would be used frequently but in small quantities: culinary herbs; tomatoes and green onions for salads and garnishes; strawberries and apples, or pears, for special desserts; and productive annuals for colorful bouquets. The smaller bed features additional flowers for cutting, though some of this space can be converted to vegetables, using the alternative selections. Good, well-drained soil, routine garden watering, and full sun during the growing season will give you a flourishing kitchen garden in zones 5 through 9 and dry-summer zone 10. Choose the fruit tree, strawberry, and tomato cultivars that will be best suited to your particular climate.

Maintenance is concentrated in late winter and early spring: a little pruning and trimming plus replacement of annual plants and any herbs that may have perished over the winter. Prune the espaliered fruit tree as needed to maintain its form. Cut back by up to half the garden sage, oregano, and thymes. When soil is workable, set out green onion starts, parsley seedlings, and pot marigolds; set out the tomatoes, sweet basil, African and French marigolds, zinnia, and snapdragon when soil has warmed. In the larger bed, switch the tomatoes and annual flowers each year to avoid growing tomatoes in the same soil year after year. When the strawberries, Shasta daisies, and chives become too crowded and unproductive, divide and replant them in early spring. During the growing season, watch the espaliered fruit tree's growth: Train new growth that will fit the formal espalier pattern and cut out wayward stems.

Variations

If the double-bed plan doesn't suit your space or needs, plant only the larger rectangle with its assortment of edibles and flowers. If you want the two beds but prefer more vegetables, consider the small-bed options in the alternative selections list, substituting zucchini and crookneck squash for the orange and yellow pot marigolds.

Malus pumila (apple)

Thymus vulgaris (common thyme)

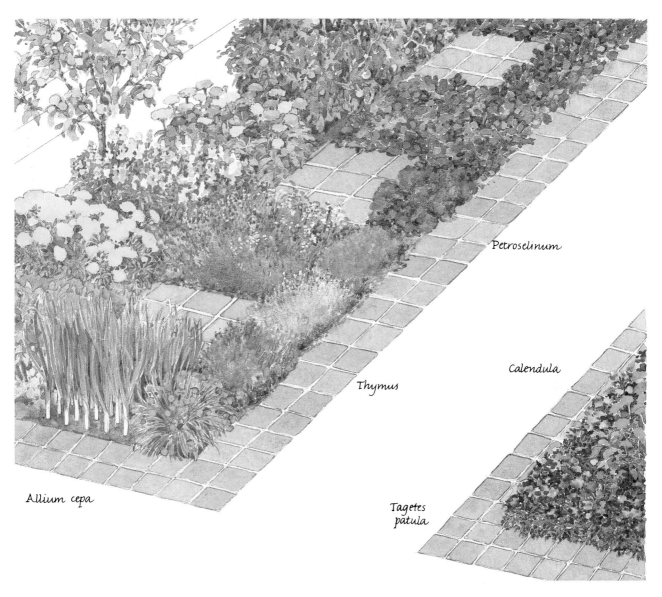

Petroselinum

Thymus

Allium cepa

Calendula

Tagetes
patula

Calendula officinalis
(pot marigold)

Cucurbita pepo (zucchini)

Kitchen-Garden Plants

A. *Malus pumila* (apple) or *Pyrus communis* (pear), espaliered tree on dwarfing rootstock (1)
B. *Fragaria × ananassa* (strawberry) (5)
C. *Salvia officinalis* (garden sage) (1)
D. *Allium schoenoprasum* (chives) (6)
E. *Thymus vulgaris* (common thyme) (1)
    Thymus vulgaris 'Argenteus' (silver thyme) (1)
    Thymus × citriodorus (lemon thyme) (1)
F. *Origanum vulgare* (oregano) (2)
G. *Petroselinum crispum* (parsley) (12)
H. *Ocimum basilicum* (sweet basil) (4)
I. *Allium cepa* (green onion) (18)
J. *Lycopersicon lycopersicum* (tomato) (2)
K. *Tagetes erecta* (African marigold) (6)
    Antirrhinum majus (snapdragon) (6)
    Zinnia elegans (zinnia) (6)
L. *Tagetes patula* (French marigold) (36)
M. *Chrysanthemum × superbum* (Shasta daisy) (6)
N. *Calendula officinalis*, orange selection (pot marigold) (6)
O. *Calendula officinalis*, yellow selection (pot marigold) (6)

Alternative Selections

N. *Cucurbita pepo* (zucchini) (1)
O. *Cucurbita pepo* (crookneck squash) (1)

Allium cepa (green onion)

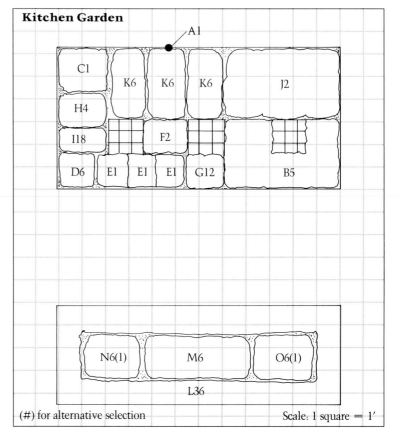

Kitchen Garden

(#) for alternative selection   Scale: 1 square = 1'

A CUTTING GARDEN

Few things in everyday life are as uplifting as a bouquet of fresh flowers. And what, then, could be more satisfying than picking them from your own garden? Although you can cut virtually any flower for the house, not all are endowed with what is known as good vase life. The annuals and perennials in this planting scheme are both attractive and fairly long lasting as cut flowers. The bells-of-Ireland, sea-lavender, fernleaf yarrow, baby's-breath, and strawflower selections even can be harvested and dried for later use as components of ever-lasting floral arrangements.

In spring, the garden will offer calendulas, snapdragons, and Shasta daisies, but the flowering peak occurs in midsummer when virtually the entire cutting garden bed will be bursting with bright color. Flowering continues into fall until the first frost with various daisies, such as purple coneflower and heliopsis. The alternative selections are options for varying the color of the garden. With one exception, the plants in both lists will grow in zones 4 through 9 and dry-summer zone 10. The exception is the border carnation, which you may need to treat as an annual in zones 4, 5, and 6, since it probably won't survive the winters in those zones. Be sure to place this cutting garden in full sun and give it "vegetable garden care"—good soil and a regular water supply during the growing season.

This garden's yearly maintenance starts in late winter or early spring, when you need to first clear the garden of last year's spent annual plants and the old flowering stems and dead leaves of the perennials. Where the annuals had been, dig the soil, adding a little fertilizer and new organic amendments. Then, when the frost danger has passed, set out new annuals. Among the perennials, the baby's-breath can remain in place permanently. But about every three years in early spring, you will need to dig and divide the coneflowers, fernleaf yarrow, and heliopsis. The Shasta daisy may need dividing every other year. Even in the zones where the border carnation will live over from year to year, periodically you'll need to start new plants from cuttings when the old plants become woody and less productive.

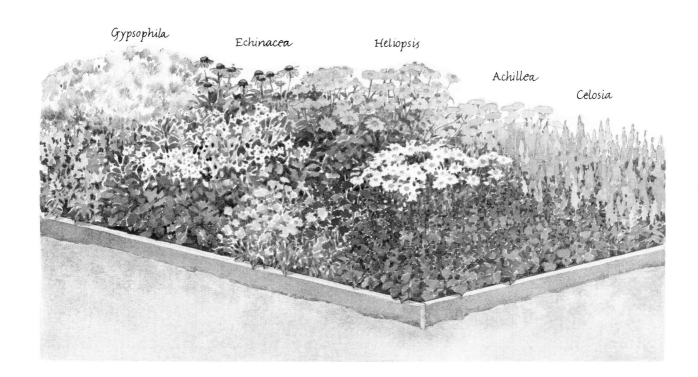

Cutting-Garden Plants

A. *Gypsophila paniculata* 'Bristol Fairy' (baby's-breath) (1)
B. *Echinacea purpurea* (purple coneflower) (4)
C. *Achillea filipendulina* 'Coronation Gold' (fernleaf yarrow) (4)
D. *Heliopsis helianthoides scabra* (heliopsis) (2)
E. *Chrysanthemum × superbum* (Shasta daisy) (4)
F. *Dianthus caryophyllus* (border carnation) (2)
G. *Nicotiana alata* (flowering tobacco) (6)
H. *Antirrhinum majus* (snapdragon) (6)
I. *Limonium sinuatum* (sea-lavender) (6)
J. *Salvia splendens*, purple selection (scarlet sage) (6)
K. *Tagetes*, triploid hybrid (triploid marigold) (8)
L. *Moluccella laevis* (bells-of-Ireland) (4)
M. *Zinnia elegans* (zinnia) (6)
N. *Calendula officinalis* (pot marigold) (6)
O. *Tagetes patula* (French marigold) (6)
P. *Celosia cristata* 'Plumosa' (cockscomb) (6)
Q. *Salvia splendens*, red selection (scarlet sage) (8)

Alternative Selections

B. *Rudbeckia fulgida* 'Goldsturm' (coneflower) (4)
D. *Cosmos sulphureus*, Klondike strain (yellow cosmos) (2)
J. *Cosmos sulphureus*, Dwarf Klondike strain (yellow cosmos) (4)
L. *Helichrysum bracteatum* (strawflower) (6)
N. *Gaillardia pulchella* (gaillardia) (6)

Nicotiana alata (flowering tobacco)

During the flowering season, routinely remove any spent flowers left on the plants after cuttings for bouquets have been taken; this prevents the plants from setting seed, which causes a decline in bloom production.

Variations

Since a cutting garden is essentially a flower factory, these rectangular plant units are perfect for easy care and cutting (and avoid the row-crop look of a vegetable garden). This setup also makes it easy to alter the garden's size by simply eliminating certain blocks of plants. You could, for example, cut out the marigolds and scarlet sage, or the alternative yellow cosmos, to gain a shorter bed. Or to create a nearly square bed, you might want to eliminate the blocks of Shasta daisy, border carnation, scarlet sage, cockscomb, French marigold, and one third of the pot marigold. Many other alterations can be made by slightly changing the numbers of plants in a block.

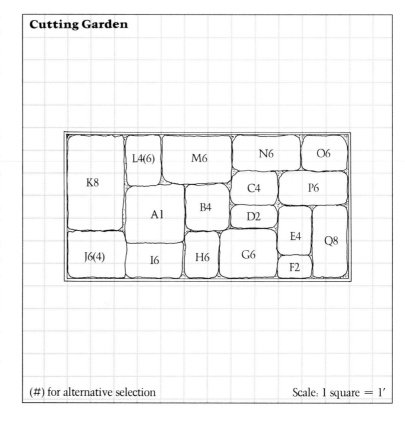

Cutting Garden

K8
L4(6)
M6
N6
O6
C4
P6
A1
B4
D2
E4
Q8
J6(4)
I6
H6
G6
F2

(#) for alternative selection

Scale: 1 square = 1'

A SHADE GARDEN

Gardeners often regard a shaded garden as a limitation, knowing that it is a poor location for such favorites as roses, irises, peonies, and a host of seasonal annuals. However, the notion of shade as a problem can be dispelled by expanded horizons and experience. Welcome to this shade garden's world of azaleas, hostas, and astilbes!

There are various types and degrees of shade. Dappled or filtered shade is the lightest—that which comes through lattice or an open-structured tree. At the other extreme is the dense shade found under a heavy foliage canopy. Shade varies from partial (morning sun, afternoon shade) to total. Even total shade varies in degree—from the fairly light kind cast by shadows of tall trees or buildings to the gloom in a narrow passage between buildings. The beds here receive their shade from the canopies of the dogwoods (or evergreen pears) included in the planting scheme. In an already shady spot, you can leave out the trees without affecting the design. The main plant list will serve zones 5 through 9, though gardeners in the warmer zones 7 and 8 can choose from the broad range of azaleas available in local nurseries. The alternative selections should be used in zone 10 and may be considered for zone 9 gardens. The alternative azaleas, in particular, are more suitable for zone 9 gardens than the azaleas on the main list. In all areas, see that the planting receives routine garden watering.

The varied colors of the foliage as well as the flowers make this planting attractive from early spring into fall, until frost spells an end to the growing year. Lenten-roses and violets usher in the flowering season, followed by the azaleas, brunnera, common bleeding heart, bloodroot, and foxglove. In late spring and summer, the Serbian bellflower, astilbe, and summersweet provide a burst of color; and the plantain lilies flower, although most are not especially showy. Overhead, the kousa dogwoods spread clouds of color. The season finishes in fall with the Japanese anemone and the colorful foliage of the azalea and dogwood.

The time for maintenance is late winter or early spring, as soon as you can get into the garden before the year's growth begins in earnest. Clean out the dead leaves and cut down the spent flowering stems of last year's perennials. Prune the summersweet if it is growing out of bounds or, if you are using the alternative list, cut back the hydrangea by at least half. Wait until just after flowering to shape the azaleas. If the Serbian bellflower, Japanese anemone, or brunnera are spreading too far, dig out the excess plants. If the dead nettle becomes patchy, dig, divide, and replant.

Variations

This shaded garden is planned as a woodland walk, perhaps along a mossy stone path. However, if your space is limited, either half of the planting can stand by itself as a solo bed.

Top: *Aquilegia* (columbine)
Bottom: *Clivia miniata* (Kaffir-lily)

Viola

Shade-Garden Plants

A. *Cornus kousa* (kousa dogwood) (2)
B. *Rhododendron vaseyi* (pink-shell azalea) (2)
C. *Rhododendron schlippenbachii* (azalea) (4)
D. *Rhododendron*, Northern Lights hybrid (azalea) (3)
E. *Clethra alnifolia* (summersweet) (1)
F. *Matteuccia struthiopteris* (ostrich fern) (4)
G. *Helleborus orientalis* (Lenten-rose) (7)
H. *Hosta sieboldiana* (plantain lily) (3)
I. *Digitalis* × *mertonensis* (foxglove) (10)
J. *Hosta undulata* (wavyleaf plantain lily) (10)
K. *Astilbe* × 'Red Sentinel' (false-spiraea) (2)
L. *Brunnera macrophylla* (brunnera) (7)
M. *Dicentra spectabilis* (common bleeding heart) (6)
N. *Hosta* × 'Piedmont Gold' (plantain lily) (1)
O. *Lamium maculatum* 'White Nancy' (dead nettle) (7)
P. *Viola odorata* (sweet violet) (4)
Q. *Ligularia dentata* 'Desdemona' (ligularia) (2)
R. *Campanula poscharskyana* (Serbian bellflower) (8)
S. *Sanguinaria canadensis* (bloodroot) (2)
T. *Anemone* × *hybrida* (Japanese anemone) (4)

Alternative Selections

A. *Pyrus kawakamii* (evergreen pear) (2)
B. *Rhododendron* × 'George Lindley Taber' (azalea) (2)
C. *Rhododendron* × 'Alaska' (azalea) (4)
D. *Rhododendron* × 'Sherwood Orchid' (azalea) (3)
E. *Hydrangea macrophylla* 'Tricolor' (bigleaf hydrangea) (1)
F. *Nephrolepis cordifolia* (southern sword fern) (5)
H. *Clivia miniata* (Kaffir-lily) (3)
J. *Liriope muscari* 'Variegata' (big blue lily-turf) (12)
K. *Anemone* × *hybrida* (Japanese anemone) (3)
M. *Aquilegia*, McKana Giants strain (columbine) (10)
N. *Zantedeschia aethiopica* 'Minor' (common calla) (3)
Q. *Ligularia tussilaginea* (ligularia) (2)
S. *Primula* × *polyantha* (polyanthus primrose) (5)

Rhododendron vaseyi (pink-shell azalea)

Dicentra spectabilis (common bleeding heart)

Helleborus

Brunnera

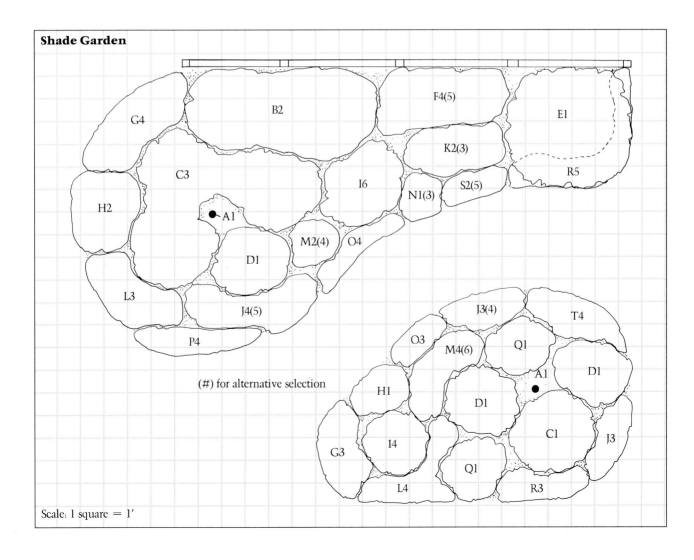

Shade Garden

G4

B2

F4(5)

E1

C3

K2(3)

I6

R5

H2

N1(3) S2(5)

● A1

M2(4)   O4

D1

L3

J4(5)

P4

J3(4)   T4

O3   M4(6)   Q1

(#) for alternative selection

H1   D1   A1   D1
●

G3   I4   C1   J3

Q1

L4   R3

Scale: 1 square = 1′

Perovskia   *Echinacea*   *Berberis*   *Rudbeckia*

A WATER-THRIFTY GARDEN

Many of our favorite garden plants need a regular supply of water to look their best. If rainfall during the growing season doesn't provide enough, you must supplement with routine watering to keep the plants in tip-top shape. But this poses a problem if you can't always be there when needed with the hose or if you're trying to conserve water. What a pleasure, then, it would be to have a bed of attractive plants that flourish on limited water.

This planting scheme features an assortment of water-thrifty plants that will thrive in zones 5 through 9; gardeners in dry-summer zone 10 should use the alternative selections, and gardeners in dry-summer zone 9 may choose from either list. Most of the color comes from the flowers, but three plants—Japanese barberry, lamb's-ears, and fountaingrass—offer colored foliage rather than showy blossoms. In the main planting, flowers are concentrated in summer and early fall. A garden containing the alternative selections will have a slightly longer flowering period. It will start flowering in spring with the rockrose, bush morning glory, and Mexican daisy and continue well into fall with the Mexican bush sage.

In all areas, establish the bed in well-drained soil where plants will receive full sun.

Although these plants can take some dryness between waterings, just how much water they'll need depends on your particular climate: temperature, rainfall, wind, and cloud cover. You can be sure, however, that they'll be standing tall when your roses, snapdragons, and lawn start to droop.

A basic spring cleaning (in late winter or early spring) gets the garden set for the year. Clear out the dead leaves, and cut down the spent flower stems on the perennials. Cut back the catmint and English lavender by about half, and cut back the Russian sage to about 6 inches. Lightly prune the redleaf Japanese barberry as needed to keep it from encroaching on neighboring plants. After several years, as the plants become crowded, you will need to dig and divide the following perennials in early spring—fernleaf yarrow, both of the coneflowers, Cupid's-dart, lamb's-ears, Moonshine yarrow, and coreopsis.

Variations

If space is limited, you can cut the planting in half. Draw a line from the back of the bed to the front between the fernleaf yarrow and the redleaf Japanese barberry; plant the half that contains the fernleaf yarrow, reducing the numbers of Cupid's-dart (or the alternative vervain) to three and lamb's-ears also to three.

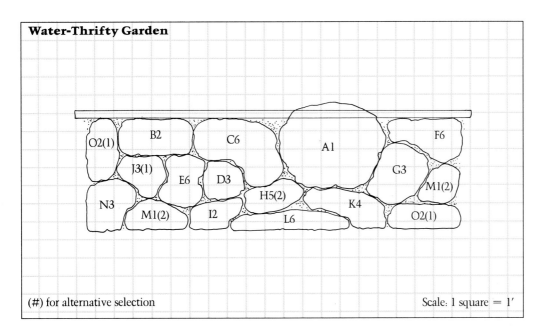

Water-Thrifty Garden

(#) for alternative selection   Scale: 1 square = 1'

Erigeron karvinskianus (Mexican daisy)

Water-Thrifty Garden Plants

A. *Berberis thunbergii* 'Atropurpurea' (redleaf Japanese barberry) (1)
B. *Perovskia atriplicifolia* (Russian sage) (2)
C. *Achillea filipendulina* 'Coronation Gold' (fernleaf yarrow) (6)
D. *Pennisetum alopecuroides* (Chinese pennisetum) (3)
E. *Echinacea purpurea* 'Bright Star' (purple coneflower) (6)
F. *Rudbeckia fulgida* 'Goldsturm' (coneflower) (6)
G. *Asclepias tuberosa* (butterfly weed) (3)
H. *Catananche caerulea* (Cupid's-dart) (5)
I. *Euphorbia epithymoides* (*E. polychroma*) (cushion spurge) (2)
J. *Liatris spicata* 'Kobold' (gayfeather) (3)
K. *Achillea* × 'Moonshine' (yarrow) (4)
L. *Stachys byzantina* 'Silver Carpet' (lamb's-ears) (6)
M. *Potentilla* × 'Abbotswood' (cinquefoil) (2)
N. *Coreopsis lanceolata* × 'Goldfink' (coreopsis) (3)
O. *Nepeta* × *faassenii* (catmint) (4)

Alternative Selections

A. *Cistus ladanifer* (crimson-spot rockrose) (1)
B. *Salvia leucantha* (Mexican bush sage) (2)
D. *Pennisetum setaceum* 'Cupreum' (fountaingrass) (3)
G. *Gaura lindheimeri* (gaura) (3)
H. *Verbena rigida* (vervain) (2)
I. *Limonium latifolium* (sea-lavender) (2)
J. *Convolvulus cneorum* (bush morning glory) (1)
M. *Lavandula angustifolia* 'Hidcote' (English lavender) (4)
O. *Erigeron karvinskianus* (Mexican daisy) (2)

Achillea × 'Moonshine' (yarrow)

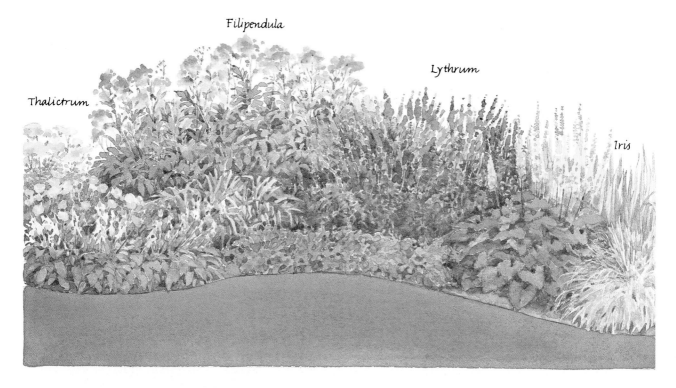

A DAMP-SOIL GARDEN

Most familiar garden plants thrive in well-drained soil; during active growth their roots need abundant air. Soil that remains damp maintains a low air-to-moisture ratio—the reason many gardeners regard damp soil as a problem. However, there's another way of looking at a patch of damp soil: It gives you the opportunity to grow a select company of plants that perform well only with abundant moisture during the growing season.

This planting includes some of the most attractive moisture-loving plants. Flowering begins in early to mid-spring with the forget-me-not and lasts into fall with the beebalm (or the alternative New England aster). Never an eye-jolting blast of mass color, this bed is nonetheless always interesting; its varied foliage textures and colors are punctuated by flowers in yellow, red, pink, purple, and blue. The alternative selections give you the chance to vary the planting color.

In cool-summer regions, place the bed in full sun; but in warmer areas, see that it receives light or filtered shade during the hottest part of the day. Because damp soil is found most frequently in climates where rain falls during the spring and summer growing seasons, these plants were chosen for moist-summer zones 5 through 9 (including the Pacific Northwest west of the Cascades). Gardeners in the dry-summer regions get more value for their water by landscaping with other low-water-use plants.

In late winter or early spring, before the perennials break dormancy, go over the bed, removing the dead leaves and spent flowering stems from the previous year. After several years you may need to dig up and divide the beebalm, lobelia, and New England aster.

Variations

This bed was designed to be an irregular island, perhaps surrounded by lawn in the low spot of a garden. However, if you need an irregular bed that will fit against a wall or fence, draw a line between the dots at either end of the plan and plant the larger half, using just half the specified number of yellow flag.

Damp-Soil Garden Plants

A. *Filipendula rubra* 'Venusta' (queen-of-the-prairie) (2)

B. *Iris pseudacorus* (yellow flag) (4)

C. *Ligularia stenocephala* 'The Rocket' (ligularia) (1)

D. *Ligularia dentata* 'Desdemona' (ligularia) (1)

E. *Lythrum virgatum* 'Dropmore Purple' (purple loosestrife) (2)

F. *Lobelia cardinalis* (cardinal flower) (3)

G. *Thalictrum aquilegifolium* (meadow rue) (2)

H. *Trollius europaeus* 'Superbus' (globeflower) (5)

I. *Monarda didyma* 'Violet Queen' (beebalm) (2)

J. *Tradescantia* × *andersoniana* (*T. virginiana*) (spiderwort) (2)

K. *Molinia caerulea* 'Variegata' (variegated purple moorgrass) (8)

L. *Myosotis scorpioides* (forget-me-not) (10)

M. *Hosta sieboldiana* (plantain lily) (4)

N. *Hosta lancifolia* (narrowleaf plantain lily) (3)

Alternative Selections

A. *Aruncus dioicus* (goatsbeard) (2)

C. *Aster novae-angliae* (New England aster) (3)

E. *Lythrum virgatum* 'Morden Pink' (purple loosestrife) (2)

I. *Monarda didyma* 'Cambridge Scarlet' (beebalm) (2)

Ligularia stenocephala 'The Rocket' (ligularia)

Damp-Soil Garden

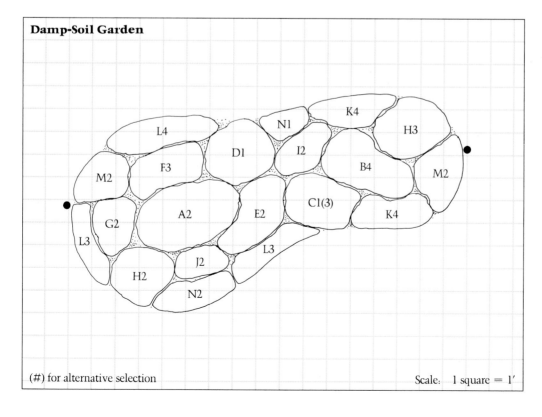

(#) for alternative selection

Scale: 1 square = 1′

A POND GARDEN

From ancient times, water has been an essential element in pleasure gardens. Now, as then,
its effect is more than just a sense of coolness:
Water is able to soothe or pacify, even impart
a sense of rejuvenation. And it doesn't take a
great body of water to accomplish this. The
Persians, Moorish Arabs, and Japanese all
were masters of effect with small pools and
channels, often employing the sound of moving
or splashing water to enhance the impression
of peacefulness.

This pond garden, then, is deliberately
small—a tranquil pool in a garden corner. The
plants complement the restful scene rather
than distract with flamboyant flowers, and if
not pond-edge denizens at least look as though
they could be. Plants in the main list are suited
to zones 5 through 9. The alternative selections
should be chosen for zone 10 gardens and can
be used as options in zone 9. Where summers

are cool, the planting will thrive in full sun, but
in warm- to hot-summer regions, give it a little
light or dappled shade at least during the hottest part of the day. In all areas, see that the
plants receive routine watering to supplement
rainfall.

When gardening weather returns in late
winter or early spring, clean up the dead
leaves, and cut back last year's feather reedgrass foliage before new growth begins. You
can leave most of the plants in place for many
years with no attention beyond cleanup and
watering. But when the carpet-bugle and dead
nettle become patchy, dig, divide, and replant
in early spring.

Variations

If you have a smaller space and want more of
the pool margin exposed, you can eliminate the
shorter "arm" by stopping the planting where
the ligularia meets the yellow flag.

Pond Garden

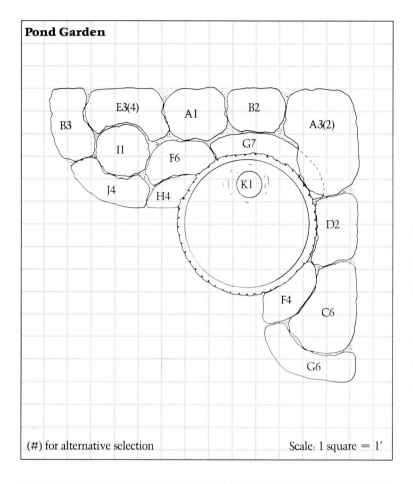

(#) for alternative selection   Scale: 1 square = 1'

Hosta gracillima 'Variegata' (variegated plantain lily)

Pond-Garden Plants

A. *Calamagrostis × acutiflora* 'Stricta' (feather reedgrass) (4)
B. *Bergenia cordifolia* (heartleaf bergenia) (5)
C. *Iris pseudacorus* (yellow flag) (6)
D. *Ligularia dentata* 'Desdemona' (ligularia) (2)
E. *Matteuccia struthiopteris* (ostrich fern) (3)
F. *Hakonechloa macra* 'Aureola' (Japanese forestgrass) (10)
G. *Hosta gracillima* 'Variegata' (variegated plantain lily) (13)
H. *Ajuga reptans* (carpet-bugle) (4)
I. *Hosta* × 'Piedmont Gold' (plantain lily) (1)
J. *Lamium maculatum* 'White Nancy' (dead nettle) (4)
K. *Pontederia cordata* (pickerelweed) (1)

Alternative Selections

A. *Nandina domestica* (heavenly-bamboo) (3)
B. *Bergenia crassifolia* (winter-blooming bergenia) (5)
D. *Ligularia tussilaginea* (ligularia) (2)
E. *Nephrolepis cordifolia* (southern sword fern) (4)
F. *Acorus gramineus* 'Variegatus' (variegated sweet flag) (10)
G. *Ophiopogon japonicus* (mondograss) (13)
I. *Clivia miniata* (Kaffir-lily) (1)

Ajuga reptans (carpet-bugle)

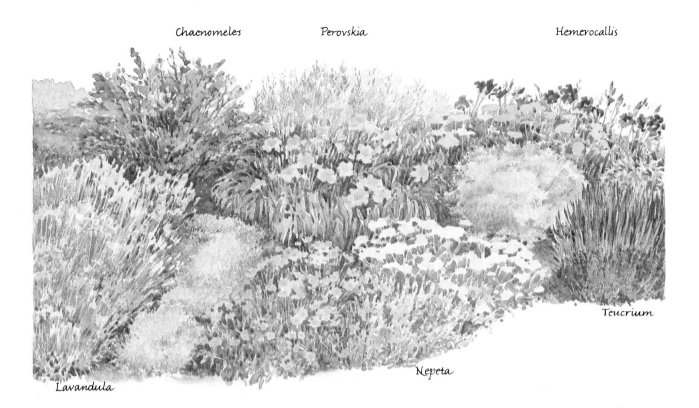

Chaenomeles   Perovskia   Hemerocallis

Teucrium

Nepeta

Lavandula

A HILLSIDE GARDEN

When a garden changes levels, there is always the problem of the slope. Do you settle for a mediocre lawn, go to the expense of terracing, or go for the monotonous verdure of juniper or ivy? Fortunately, there are a number of good-looking garden plants that are well suited to life on a hillside—and this plan assembles some of the best into a bed that will make the topographical transition worth looking at.

Water penetrates poorly on sloping ground; some of it runs off before it soaks in. And sloping land frequently is composed of shallow or poor soil, especially if the slope is a land cut. Consequently, a good hillside plant has to be a tough one, able to thrive in marginal soils with something less than routine garden watering. All these plants are equal to that challenge. However, to give them a chance to look their best, you should dig the soil well before planting and then water carefully and regularly until the planting is established. Be sure this hillside bed will receive sun for at least three fourths of the day.

The main planting list is for zones 6 through 9; in zones 6 and 7, the variegated common sage may perish in exceptionally cold winters, but spring replacement plants will fill in quickly. The alternative selections should be used in dry-summer zone 10 and may be chosen for gardens in dry-summer zone 9.

The flowering quince kicks off the color display in late winter or early spring, when its bare branches deck themselves in pink or red flowers. After it has finished blooming, it becomes a twiggy, leafy backdrop to its summer-flowering neighbors. The main planting scheme is at its most colorful from early to late summer, beginning with the Vancouver Gold broom. Among the alternative selections, the feathery cassia flowers in late winter and early spring, the rockrose and two morning glories bloom in spring, and the Mexican bush sage puts on a lavish purple display in late summer and fall.

To maintain this garden, go over it in late winter or early spring with shears in hand. On the perennials, cut out all the dead stems that bore last year's flowers. Cut back the Russian sage and blue-mist to about 6 inches. Cut back halfway the English lavender, southernwood, common wormwood, variegated common sage, and catmint. To keep the plants compact, shear back as needed the broom, lavender-cotton, and

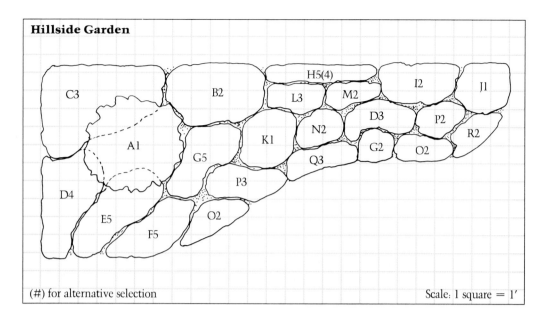

Hillside Garden

C3

B2

H5(4)

I2

J1

L3

M2

A1

K1

N2

D3

P2

R2

G5

Q3

G2

O2

D4

P3

E5

O2

F5

(#) for alternative selection

Scale: 1 square = 1'

germander. If they won't be unsightly, you might want to leave the dead leaves in place as the basis for a mulch. Mulches aid water penetration, retard evaporation, and moderate soil temperature—three characteristics that particularly benefit plants growing on a hillside. After several years, you may need to dig up and divide the two kinds of yarrow and coreopsis if the plantings are crowded.

Variations

If the maximum planting depth of 10 feet is greater than you need, you can reduce it to 7 feet. Below the flowering quince, eliminate the English lavender, lavender-cotton, *Coreopsis lanceolata*, and catmint. Add one more plant of broom (or the alternative sageleaf rockrose) to finish off the new edge.

Hillside-Garden Plants
A. *Chaenomeles* × 'Cameo' or 'Texas Scarlet' (flowering quince) (1)
B. *Perovskia atriplicifolia* (Russian sage) (2)
C. *Genista pilosa* 'Vancouver Gold' (broom) (3)
D. *Lavandula angustifolia* (English lavender) (7)
E. *Santolina chamaecyparissus* (lavender-cotton) (5)
F. *Coreopsis lanceolata* (coreopsis) (5)
G. *Hemerocallis*, dark yellow cultivar (daylily) (7)
H. *Hemerocallis*, red cultivar (daylily) (5)
I. *Caryopteris* × *clandonensis* (blue-mist) (2)
J. *Artemisia abrotanum* (southernwood) (1)
K. *Artemisia absinthium* (common wormwood) (1)
L. *Achillea filipendulina* 'Coronation Gold' (fernleaf yarrow) (3)
M. *Salvia officinalis* 'Icterina' (variegated garden sage) (2)
N. *Imperata cylindrica* 'Rubra' (Japanese bloodgrass) (2)
O. *Nepeta* × *faassenii* (catmint) (4)
P. *Achillea* × 'Moonshine' (yarrow) (5)
Q. *Teucrium chamaedrys* (germander) (3)
R. *Coreopsis verticillata* 'Zagreb' (coreopsis) (2)

Alternative Selections
A. *Cassia artemisioides* (feathery cassia) (1)
B. *Salvia leucantha* (Mexican bush sage) (2)
C. *Cistus salviifolius* (sageleaf rockrose) (3)
H. *Agapanthus orientalis* (lily-of-the-Nile) (4)
I. *Convolvulus cneorum* (bush morning glory) (2)
Q. *Convolvulus mauritanicus* (ground morning glory) (3)

Hemerocallis 'New Yorker' (daylily)

Tithonia

Salvia

Gaillardia

AN ANNUALS GARDEN

Evaluated in flowers per square foot, no other planting quite matches the output of a bed of annuals. Give these plants just the sort of care you would give a garden of vegetables, and you'll have nonstop color throughout most of the growing season. Their rapid growth to flowering size nearly puts them into the "instant landscape" category, a point especially appreciated by the new homeowner facing a bare expanse of soil, and by any gardener with limited space. Another virtue of annuals is their great adaptability. Many of the popular kinds will thrive in diverse climates. The petunias, for example, that you see on Cape Cod are the same kind as you might find in Omaha and Phoenix.

This garden focuses on warm-season or summer annuals that give the longest-running performance. The flowers will thrive in all parts of zones 3 through 10 except the humid-summer part of zone 10 and the high-latitude regions where summers are both cool and short. The main plant list features bright colors including orange and gold shades; the alternative selections replace strident colors with softer tones plus pink, rose, and magenta. Select a garden

Coreopsis tinctoria (annual coreopsis)

Tagetes

Cosmos

Mirabilis

spot in full sun, then prepare the soil as you would for a vegetable plot, digging in organic amendments and fertilizer. Set out young started plants when there is no longer any danger of frost and preferably when the soil has warmed a little.

During the growing season, your maintenance work should be aimed at keeping the plants growing actively. Water as often as needed during spring and summer. Just as with vegetables, you keep productivity up by maintaining steady growth unhindered by periods of drought. It's also a good idea to remove spent flowers periodically. This keeps the plants from diverting their energies from flower production to seed setting. When colder weather or frost spells an end to the flowering season, you have two choices: Remove the plants or leave them in place over winter. In colder regions—especially where snow falls—you might leave them in place since the untidy appearance of the garden in winter will be less of an issue, and birds may appreciate any seeds that form from the last set of flowers. In late winter or early spring, when the soil is workable, dig or till the bed, replenish organic amendments and fertilizers, and prepare for another planting season.

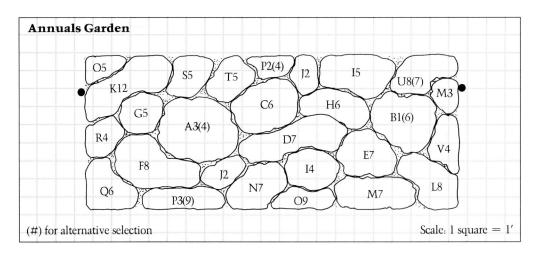

Annuals Garden

(#) for alternative selection   Scale: 1 square = 1'

Annuals-Garden Plants

A. *Tithonia rotundifolia* (Mexican sunflower) (3)
B. *Mirabilis jalapa* (four-o'clock) (1)
C. *Tagetes erecta*, yellow selection (African marigold) (6)
D. *Cosmos sulphureus*, Klondike strain (yellow cosmos) (7)
E. *Zinnia elegans*, red, orange, or yellow selection (zinnia) (7)
F. *Tagetes erecta*, orange selection (African marigold) (8)
G. *Salvia splendens*, purple selection (scarlet sage) (5)
H. *Coreopsis tinctoria* (annual coreopsis) (6)
I. *Dahlia*, bedding, bronze-leafed selection (9)
J. *Euphorbia marginata* (snow-on-the-mountain) (4)
K. *Calendula officinalis*, cream selection (pot marigold) (12)
L. *Celosia cristata* 'Plumosa', gold selection (cockscomb) (8)
M. *Ageratum houstonianum* (flossflower) (10)
N. *Nicotiana alata* 'Lime Green' (flowering tobacco) (7)
O. *Lobularia maritima* (sweet alyssum) (14)
P. *Sanvitalia procumbens* (creeping zinnia) (5)
Q. *Petunia* × *hybrida*, blue selection (petunia) (6)
R. *Gaillardia pulchella* (gaillardia) (4)
S. *Moluccella laevis* (bells-of-Ireland) (5)
T. *Salvia splendens*, lavender selection (scarlet sage) (5)
U. *Zinnia haageana* (zinnia) (8)
V. *Petunia* × *hybrida*, yellow selection (petunia) (4)

Alternative Selections

A. *Cleome spinosa* 'Helen Campbell' (spiderflower) (4)
B. *Lavatera trimestris* (annual mallow) (6)
C. *Tagetes erecta*, light yellow selection (African marigold) (6)
D. *Cosmos bipinnatus* 'Candystripe' (cosmos) (7)
E. *Zinnia elegans*, magenta selection (zinnia) (7)
F. *Tagetes erecta*, yellow selection (African marigold) (8)
H. *Scabiosa atropurpurea* (pincushion-flower) (6)
I. *Dahlia*, bedding, cream or yellow selection (9)
N. *Nicotiana alata* 'Nicki Rose' (flowering tobacco) (7)
P. *Phlox drummondii* (annual phlox) (13)
R. *Catharanthus roseus*, white (Madagascar periwinkle) (4)
U. *Limonium bonduellii* (sea-lavender) (7)

Variations

This planting, which is 8 feet deep, was designed as an island bed accessible from all sides. If you want a shallower bed to plant against a wall or fence, you can draw a line between the dots at either end of the plan, and omit all the plants in the smaller segment. This will give you a bed of the same length but only 6 feet deep. If you choose this option, plant just 9 pot marigolds, 4 yellow (or the alternative light yellow) African marigolds, and 2 flossflowers.

Nicotiana alata (flowering tobacco)

Cleome spinosa 'Helen Campbell' (spiderflower)

Heuchera   Geranium

A PERENNIALS GARDEN

A garden of perennials soon becomes a reunion of faithful old friends. Each year they reappear at their appointed times, mingle graciously, then depart one by one—leaving you with the cleanup! Nonetheless, an annual tidying is a small price to pay for the bountiful flowers perennials produce year after year. You can leave most perennials in place for many years before they will need replanting to restore their energies; others are permanent.

This garden of perennials contains some all-time favorites as well as a few less widely known kinds whose virtues should be better appreciated. The display will be summer long, starting actually in late spring with the Siberian iris and concluding in fall with the aster, stonecrop, sundrops, and perhaps a second flowering of beardtongue and daylilies. Dominating the scene are the colewort, with airy 8-foot flower panicles, and the shrubby false-indigo. Around them are plants that offer a great variety of leaf shapes, sizes, and textures, and flowers in colors from cool to warm, pale to bright. Good, well-drained soil, sun for most of the day, and routine watering will satisfy this set of plants. The main plant list contains perennials that will succeed in zones 6 through 9, given routine watering. Gardeners in dry-summer zone 10 should plant the alternative selections; gardeners in dry-summer zone 9 may choose either list.

Prepare the planting area as though you were going to set out annuals or vegetables. Because perennials will be in place for two or more years, they greatly benefit from thorough soil preparation. Once they are planted you'll need to do a yearly cleanup of dead foliage and spent flowering stems. In warmer zones complete the cleanup in late fall or winter; where freezing winters are the rule, you can delay the work until early spring, but fall is preferable. A few of the perennials will need further trimming. In warmer zones, where catmint foliage remains alive over winter, cut back the stems by about half before spring growth starts, to keep the plants compact; among the alternative selections, cut back the artemisia by half, and lightly head back the ground morning glory and Mexican daisy as needed to keep the plants from becoming rangy. Apply an all-purpose fertilizer just as growth begins each year.

How often you need to dig up and divide perennials depends on the particular perennial, the culture it receives, and your climate (plants in the warmer zones often need more frequent dividing). Crowded clumps and declining performance are your best indicators. If you are using the main list, in two or three years you may need to replace the mallow and beard-tongue. Every three or four years, you may need to divide and replant the yarrows, Shasta daisy, sage, coreopsis, coralbells, aster, stonecrop, and sundrops. The daylilies and Siberian iris can go longer. The catmint and cranesbill are less predictable; divide and replant them, or start new plants, whenever their performance declines. Consider these as permanent plants: colewort, false-indigo, baby's-breath, balloonflower, and lady's-mantle.

If you are using the alternative selections, you may need to replace the artemisia and toadflax every four or five years (you can start new plants from cuttings). Dig, divide, and replant the dahlia about every three years—also the vervain, to keep it from overrunning its neighbors. Divide or replace the ground morning

Perennials-Garden Plants
A. *Crambe cordifolia* (colewort) (1)
B. *Baptisia australis* (false-indigo) (1)
C. *Gypsophila paniculata* 'Bristol Fairy' (baby's-breath) (1)
D. *Achillea filipendulina* 'Coronation Gold' (fernleaf yarrow) (5)
E. *Malva alcea* (mallow) (7)
F. *Chrysanthemum* × *superbum* (Shasta daisy) (12)
G. *Platycodon grandiflorus* (balloonflower) (1)
H. *Salvia* × *superba* (sage) (9)
I. *Iris*, Siberian hybrid 'Ego' (2)
J. *Geranium endressii* 'Wargrave Pink' (cranesbill) (4)
K. *Sedum spectabile* (stonecrop) (5)
L. *Hemerocallis* 'Stella de Oro' (daylily) (5)
M. *Hemerocallis* 'Bertie Ferris' or other orange-apricot miniature cultivar (daylily) (2)
N. *Hemerocallis*, tall light yellow selection (daylily) (2)
O. *Nepeta* × *faassenii* (catmint) (2)
P. *Coreopsis verticillata* 'Moonbeam' (coreopsis) (3)
Q. *Alchemilla mollis* (lady's-mantle) (3)
R. *Heuchera sanguinea* (coralbells) (4)
S. *Achillea* × 'Moonshine' (yarrow) (5)
T. *Penstemon barbatus* 'Prairie Fire' (beardtongue) (3)
U. *Oenothera fruticosa* (sundrops) (1)
V. *Aster* × *frikartii* (aster) (2)

Alternative Selections
A. *Dahlia*, bush type–yellow, bronze, or peach selection (3)
C. *Artemisia arborescens* (artemisia) (1)
E. *Gaura lindheimeri* (gaura) (3)
G. *Verbena rigida* (vervain) (2)
I. *Linaria purpurea* (toadflax) (3)
J. *Erigeron karvinskianus* (Mexican daisy) (4)
N. *Agapanthus orientalis* (lily-of-the-Nile) (2)
Q. *Convolvulus mauritanicus* (ground morning glory) (2)

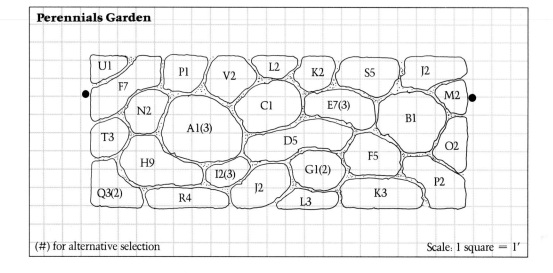

Perennials Garden

(#) for alternative selection

Scale: 1 square = 1′

glory and Mexican daisy only when reduced
vigor indicates the need. The gaura and lily-of-
the-Nile can remain undisturbed indefinitely.

Variations

This bed was designed to be viewed from all
sides. For a narrower planting to go along a
wall or fence, you can easily cut the depth from
8 feet to 6. Just draw a line connecting the dots
on either margin, then eliminate the plants in
the smaller portion. This will omit the sundrops, aster, Moonshine yarrow, Bertie Ferris
daylily, four Shasta daisies in one plant group,
and one plant group each of coreopsis, Stella de
Oro daylily, sedum, and cranesbill.

Penstemon barbatus
'Prairie Fire'
(beardtongue)

Agapanthus orientalis
(lily-of-the-Nile)

AN ORNAMENTAL-GRASSES GARDEN

No longer are grasses looked upon as just weeds or as plants to be sheared into subjugation as a lawn. The ornamental grasses—long on the periphery of horticulture—have come into the mainstream and are being recognized for their distinct beauties of form, texture, and color. This planting brings together the most commonly available grasses.

Adaptability is characteristic of these grasses. Plants in both lists will grow in zones 5 through 9 and dry-summer zone 10. The main list contains grasses that will prosper in a sunny bed; substituting the three alternative selections (including a grasslike sedge) gives you a planting you can use in light shade. Best performance, in either case, will derive from well-drained soil and routine watering.

You'll find that this bed of ornamental grasses makes relatively few maintenance demands. Aside from watering during dry periods, an annual cleanup of dead leaves and stems is the only routine to put on your schedule. All but three of the grasses (blue oatgrass, blue fescue, and tufted hairgrass) and the

Chasmanthium

Miscanthus

Calamagrostis

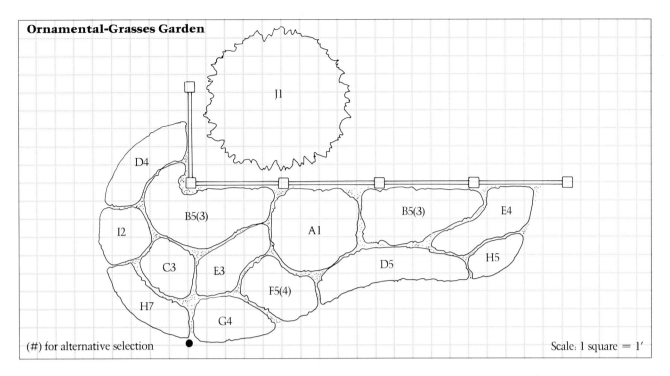

Ornamental-Grasses Garden

J1

D4

B5(3)

I2

A1

B5(3)

E4

C3

E3

D5

H5

F5(4)

H7

G4

(#) for alternative selection

Scale: 1 square = 1′

sedge are deciduous, growing an entirely new set of leaves each spring. Cleaning up deciduous grasses is simple: Cut dead material nearly to the ground. With the evergreen kinds, pull out dead leaves from the clumps (though you can give the blue fescue a close haircut when it looks unkempt). The timing for the annual cleanup depends on your climate and personal preference. The dead foliage and flower stalks may remain attractive, weather permitting, well into winter, so that you could delay cleanup, if you wished, until just before the start of new growth. In warmer areas, you could cut back dead leaves and stems any time from late fall to late winter or early spring; in snowy regions, leave all the foliage and stems through the winter. Most ornamental grasses will thrive for years without dividing and replanting. The exception in this plan is the blue fescue: When clumps decline in vigor, dig them up and replant small divisions.

Variations

Although this planting was designed to wrap around a corner, you can make a simple corner planting by cutting off the wrap. Draw a line from the corner fence post to the dot on the edge of the bed, then omit the plants in the smaller portion. Delete the purple moorgrass, sea oats, three feather reedgrass plants (or two eulalia-grass plants), and one drift of the Japanese bloodgrass and blue fescue.

Ornamental-Grasses Garden Plants
A. *Miscanthus sinensis* 'Silberfeder' (eulalia-grass) (1)
B. *Calamagrostis × acutiflora* 'Stricta' (feather reedgrass) (10)
C. *Molinia caerulea* 'Variegata' (purple moorgrass) (3)
D. *Imperata cylindrica* 'Rubra' (Japanese bloodgrass) (9)
E. *Pennisetum alopecuroides* (Chinese pennisetum) (7)
F. *Helictotrichon sempervirens* (blue oatgrass) (5)
G. *Deschampsia caespitosa* (tufted hairgrass) (4)
H. *Festuca ovina* var. *glauca* (blue fescue) (12)
I. *Chasmanthium latifolium* (sea oats) (2)
J. *Picea pungens* 'Glauca' (Colorado blue spruce) (1)

Alternative Selections
B. *Miscanthus sinensis* 'Purpurascens' (eulalia-grass) (6)
E. *Carex stricta* 'Bowles' Golden' (sedge) (7)
F. *Hakonechloa macra* 'Aureola' (Japanese forestgrass) (4)

Featured in this garden are Pennisetum alopecuroides *(Chinese pennisetum) in the foreground and* Calamagrostis × acutiflora 'Stricta' *(feather reedgrass) in the background.*

A SHRUB BORDER

Although mention of the word *shrubs* may set few gardeners' pulses racing, the vast group of plants covered by that one word includes some of the most attractive and useful garden ornaments. Shrubs also are among the best garden investments. If you choose them carefully, so that they fit their sites, they may last the lifetime of your garden. And though few shrubs offer showy flowers throughout the growing season (modern roses are a notable exception),

watering. The dominant plants are the dwarf redleaf plum and the variegated weigela, which has cream and green leaves. Both are deciduous plants, like all the other plants in this list except the germander. Foliage color is also provided by the bronze-tinted to yellow spiraea and the cranberry cotoneaster and American cranberry bush, which offer a vivid red fall foliage change. The flowering season starts in early spring with a cloud of pink blossoms on the dwarf redleaf plum; a little later in

Weigela

Prunus

Rosa

Spiraea

Potentilla

you needn't fear that a shrub border will endow your garden with the allure of an industrial park. This border shows that a selection of shrubs chosen not only for their flowers but their foliage colors and textures and their plant shapes, too, can produce a pleasingly varied garden scheme.

There are three plant lists for this border. The main plant list serves gardens in zones 6 through 9 and is suitable for a sunny location with average, well-drained soil, and routine

spring there's a burst of pink flowers on the deutzia and white flowers on the cranberry cotoneaster. The White Meidilland rose starts to flower in spring and continues blooming through fall. In late spring to summer, blooms appear on the weigela (dark rose), American cranberry bush (white), cinquefoil (yellow), spiraea (rosy red), and germander (lilac). In fall, the bright red fruits on the American cranberry bush and cranberry cotoneaster produce a final show.

Shrub Border

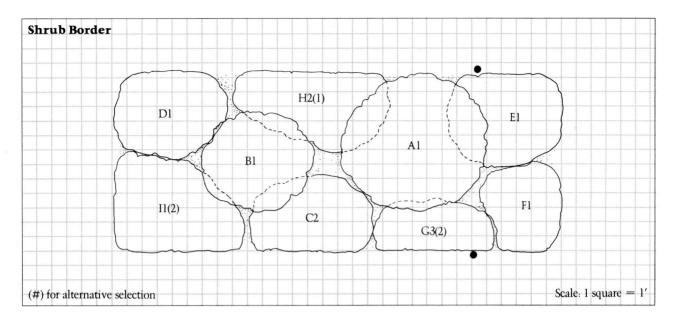

(#) for alternative selection

Scale: 1 square = 1'

The two lists of alternative selections are actually entirely different sets of shrubs from those on the main list. The first list is a mostly evergreen assortment of plants suitable for dry-summer zones 9 and 10—and average, well-drained soil in a sunny location, with moderate to routine watering. In this border the most prominent plant is the New Zealand tea-tree, which is covered with glowing crimson flowers in late winter and spring. Also flowering at this time are the dwarf rosemary, spangled with small blue blossoms; the Australian fuchsia, which produces deep red, bell-shaped flowers; the pink breath-of-heaven, a froth of tiny flowers and leaves; and the India-hawthorn, which usually starts its clusters of pink flowers in winter. In mid- to late spring, the round-leaf mint bush covers itself in a mantle of purplish blue; the dwarf carnation-flowered pomegranate brings forth its orange pompons and continues to flower through summer into fall. In summer the senecio joins the display with yellow daisies. This first list of alternatives also offers foliage variety: The senecio and bush morning glory are silvery gray; the Australian fuchsia, gray-green; the pomegranate, glossy bright green—with yellow fall color change; the New Zealand tea-tree, purple tinted; and the India-hawthorn, intensely dark green.

The second list of alternatives makes a border of winter- and spring-flowering azaleas and camellias, an excellent choice for zones 8 and 9 in the South and Southeast and zones 8, 9, and 10 on the Pacific coast. The plants will grow best in good, well-drained soil and partial

Shrub-Border Plants

A. *Prunus* × *cistena* (dwarf redleaf plum) (1)
B. *Weigela florida* 'Variegata' (variegated weigela) (1)
C. *Spiraea* × *bumalda* 'Goldflame' (spiraea) (2)
D. *Deutzia* × *rosea* (deutzia) (1)
E. *Viburnum trilobum* 'Compactum' (cranberry bush) (1)
F. *Potentilla* × 'Longacre' (cinquefoil) (1)
G. *Teucrium chamaedrys* (germander) (3)
H. *Cotoneaster apiculatus* (cranberry cotoneaster) (2)
I. *Rosa* 'White Meidilland' (1)

Alternative Selections I

A. *Leptospermum scoparium* 'Ruby Glow' (New Zealand tea-tree) (1)
B. *Raphiolepis indica* 'Pink Cloud' (India-hawthorn) (1)
C. *Senecio greyi* (senecio) (2)
D. *Prostanthera rotundifolia* (round-leaf mintbush) (1)
E. *Coleonema pulchrum* (pink breath-of-heaven) (1)
F. *Convolvulus cneorum* (bush morning glory) (1)
G. *Punica granatum* 'Chico' (dwarf carnation-flowered pomegranate) (2)
H. *Rosmarinus officinalis* 'Prostratus' (dwarf rosemary) (2)
I. *Correa* × 'Carmine Bells' (Australian fuchsia) (2)

Alternative Selections II

A. *Camellia japonica* 'Mrs. D.W. Davis' (1)
B. *Hydrangea macrophylla* 'Tricolor' (bigleaf hydrangea) (1)
C. *Rhododendron* × 'Ward's Ruby' (azalea) (2)
D. *Camellia hiemalis* 'Shishi-Gashira' (1)
E. *Rhododendron* × 'Sherwood Orchid' (azalea) (1)
F. *Rhododendron* × 'Albert and Elizabeth' (azalea) (1)
G. *Viburnum davidii* (David viburnum) (2)
H. *Rhododendron* × 'Fielder's White' (azalea) (1)
I. *Rhododendron* × 'Gumpo Pink' (azalea) (2)

Viburnum davidii
(David viburnum)

shade, with routine watering. The Shishi-Gashira camellia, a mounding plant, opens the bloom season in fall with rose red flowers that may continue into the following spring. The tall, glossy-leafed Mrs. D. W. Davis camellia opens its first blush pink, almost magnolialike flowers in mid- to late winter and continues to bloom into spring. From late winter well into spring, the chorus of azaleas builds into a colorful crescendo: first the dark rose Gumpo Pink and pink and white Albert and Elizabeth, then the aptly named Ward's Ruby, and finally the Sherwood Orchid and Fielder's White. The solo player in this border is the hydrangea. Bare in winter, it leafs out in spring with foliage variegated in gray-green and creamy white, and produces large, flat lace-cap flower clusters of tinted white in summer and early fall.

Maintenance focuses on grooming for neatness and occasional pruning to keep the plants shapely. In the main plant list, since all the plants except the germander are deciduous, it's easiest to prune in late winter and early spring because then you can easily see the plant structures. That would be the time, for example, to cut back the spiraea by about half, before its new leaves emerge in spring. However, not all the shrubs should be pruned so early. Delay pruning the rose until just after growth starts, then remove only the dead and unproductive stems. Prune the weigela only after it flowers (if you prune before, you will remove potential flower buds). Shear back the germander by about half after its flowers fade.

Since the first list of alternative plants consists of evergreens except for the pomegranate, in general it's best to prune or shape these plants after they have finished flowering. On the dwarf rosemary, New Zealand tea-tree, Australian fuchsia, and pink breath-of-heaven, don't cut back to totally leafless wood: New growth may not spring forth. If you choose the second list of alternatives, head back the hydrangea by half to two thirds while it is dormant. Shape the azaleas by pruning or shearing them just after bloom. Camellias need little pruning: Clip any wayward growth toward the end of the flowering period.

Variations

This border was designed to go along a low wall or fence. To convert it into a corner planting, with the tallest plant snuggled into the back, draw a line between the two marginal dots and eliminate the two plants in the smaller portion: American cranberry bush and cinquefoil in the main list; pink breath-of-heaven and bush morning glory in the first list of alternatives; the Sherwood Orchid and Albert and Elizabeth azaleas in the second list of alternates.

A FORMAL MODERN-ROSE GARDEN

Roses are a universally beloved flower, grown in both hemispheres and on all continents but Antarctica. From early in the nineteenth century, plant breeders have been working industriously with roses, producing the rainbow array of blossoms that we take for granted.

As it evolved in Europe, the traditional rose garden was frequently formal, often a series of rectangular units. Here is just such a formal layout, featuring the most popular classes of modern roses. The main plant list includes a sampling of the range of colors in modern roses but with a pink-red emphasis. The alternative selections feature warm yellow-orange tones.

One reason for the global popularity of roses is that, given the necessary protection from frosts and pests and diseases, roses will grow in a broad range of climates. Conceivably, you could plant this garden in any of the USDA zones, although in the coldest zones you would need to protect the plants and perhaps replace a few each spring. The common boxwood has a more limited climate tolerance than the roses, thriving just in moist- or cool-summer zones 6 through 10, although a few selections such as the Welleri and Vardar Valley common boxwoods will grow in zone 5 as well. In zones 3, 4, and 5, you can substitute the Japanese holly from the alternative selections; and in dry-summer zones 7 through 10, you can use the Japanese boxwood alternative selection. Roses appreciate good soil, sun for at least three fourths of the day, and regular watering.

For all the rewards roses give you, the extra maintenance they may need is well earned. In late winter (zones 8, 9, and 10) or early to mid-spring (colder zones) comes pruning time. Just as the new growth starts to break, you should cut out any dead or weak stems and head back the other stems both to keep the plant healthy and to encourage strong new growth that will bear the flowers. After pruning, many rose growers apply a dormant spray to kill any over-wintering fungus spores or eggs of various pests. During the growing season, water the bushes regularly to keep them healthy and productive, and apply fertilizers and spray for pests and diseases as needed. Throughout spring and summer, remove spent blossoms.

In zones 3 through 6, where freezing winter temperatures are likely to kill any exposed plants, you will want to protect your roses in late fall to ensure their survival. Some zone 7 growers also find minimal protection helpful. There are a number of ways to protect rose

Formal Modern-Rose Garden Plants

A. 'Handel' (large-flowered climber) (1)
B. 'Queen Elizabeth' (grandiflora) (4)
C. 'Mister Lincoln' (hybrid tea) (2)
D. 'Pascali' (hybrid tea) (2)
E. 'Double Delight' (hybrid tea) (3)
F. 'Miss All-American Beauty' (hybrid tea) (3)
G. 'French Lace' (floribunda) (4)
H. 'Cherish' (floribunda) (3)
I. 'Class Act' (floribunda) (4)
J. 'Angel Face' (floribunda) (4)
K. 'Over the Rainbow' (miniature) (16)
L. 'Cupcake' (miniature) (16)
M. 'Europeana' (floribunda) (13)
N. 'Amber Queen' (floribunda) (13)
O. 'Sheer Bliss' (hybrid tea) (2)
P. 'Perfume Delight' (hybrid tea) (3)
Q. 'Fragrant Cloud' (hybrid tea) (2)
R. 'Granada' (hybrid tea) (3)
S. 'Beauty Secret', standard, in container (miniature) (2)
T. *Buxus sempervirens* (common boxwood) (58)

Alternative Selections

A. 'America' (large-flowered climber) (1)
B. 'Gold Medal' (grandiflora) (4)
C. 'Duet' (hybrid tea) (2)
D. 'Dolly Parton' (hybrid tea) (2)
E. 'Peace' (hybrid tea) (2)
F. 'Chicago Peace' (hybrid tea) (3)
G. 'Charisma' (floribunda) (4)
H. 'Gingersnap' (floribunda) (3)
I. 'First Edition' (floribunda) (4)
J. 'Summer Fashion' (floribunda) (4)
K. 'Yellow Doll' (miniature) (16)
L. 'Sheri Anne' (miniature) (16)
M. 'Sun Flare' (floribunda) (13)
N. 'Showbiz' (floribunda) (13)
O. 'Prominent' (grandiflora) (2)
P. 'Brandy' (hybrid tea) (3)
Q. 'Sonia' (grandiflora) (2)
R. 'Garden Party' (hybrid tea) (3)
S. 'Rainbow's End', standard, in container (miniature) (2)
T. *Buxus microphylla* var. *japonica*, for dry-summer zones 7-10 (Japanese boxwood) (58), *Ilex glabra* 'Compacta', for zones 3-5 (Japanese holly) (40)

Rosa 'Handel'

Rosa 'Over the Rainbow'

Rosa 'Cupcake'

bushes: For example, you can mound soil around them, you can enclose them in protective cones or cylinders, or you can completely bury them. For additional specific information on winter protection and other aspects of rose care, refer to Ortho's book *All About Roses.*

Variations

This formal design comprises three separate beds that together form a unified rose garden. However, the large single bed can stand alone as an individual planting where only a more narrow space is available.

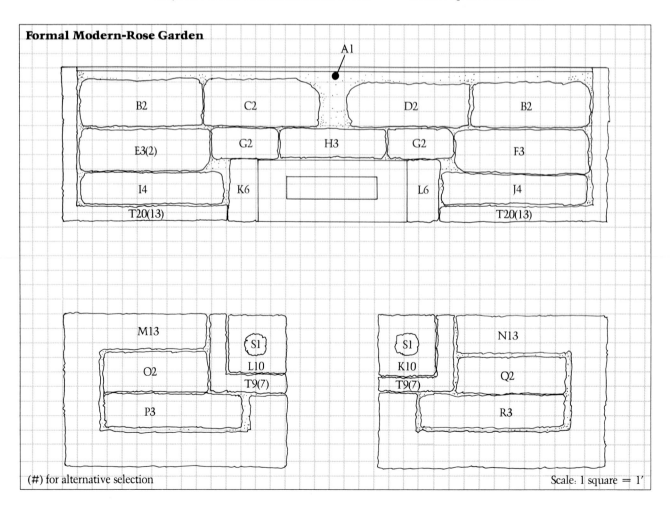

Formal Modern-Rose Garden

A1

| B2 | C2 | D2 | B2 |

| E3(2) | G2 | H3 | G2 | F3 |

| I4 | K6 | | L6 | J4 |

T20(13)　　　　　　　　　　　　　　　　T20(13)

M13　　　　　S1　　　　　S1　　　　　N13

O2　　　　　L10　　　　K10　　　　Q2
　　　　　　T9(7)　　　T9(7)

P3　　　　　　　　　　　　　　　　R3

(#) for alternative selection　　　　　　　　　　　　　　　　Scale: 1 square = 1'

AN INFORMAL MODERN-ROSE GARDEN

Although it is easy to lay out rectangular rose beds, lining up the plants in blocks like parade marchers, introducing curved lines into your plan is the best way to achieve flowing sweeps of color. The broad S-curve of this rose garden lends itself to drifts of color, and it will fit easily into a backyard corner.

This plan comprises just 11 different roses, yet they will give you garden color and cut flowers from early spring until frost. The main plant list emphasizes bright, vibrant colors: yellow, orange, bright red, and bronze shades. For a change of pace, look to the alternative selections, which concentrate on a more serene palette of white, lavender, pink shades, and rich red tones.

With winter protection in colder zones (see pages 101 to 102), this planting can be used in zones 3 through 10. Give the roses good garden soil, and plant them where they will be in sunlight for three fourths of the day or more.

A regular moisture supply is essential for keeping roses growing well throughout the flowering season. Wherever, or whenever, rainfall isn't abundant—an inch or more each week—watering your roses will be your most routine maintenance task. For other items on this garden's maintenance agenda—including pruning, pest and disease control, and winter protection—refer to the maintenance information in A Formal Modern-Rose Garden on pages 101 to 102.

Variations

If you lack sufficient space for the full S-curve, you can straighten out the front edge of the bed by drawing a line between the dots in the margins. Delete the smaller portion, eliminating the Beauty Secret (or Toy Clown) rose, Double Delight (or Sonia) rose, and one of the Class Act (or Angel Face) roses. Plant the remaining three Class Act (or Angel Face) roses in a straight line within the allotted space at the front of the bed.

Rosa 'Joseph's Coat'

Rosa 'Rainbow's End'

Rosa 'Class Act'

Informal Modern-Rose Garden

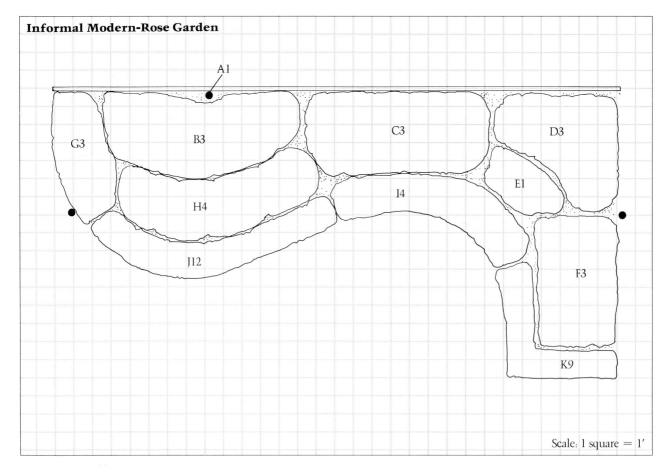

A1

G3

B3

C3

D3

E1

H4

I4

J12

F3

K9

Scale: 1 square = 1′

Rosa 'Handel'

Informal Modern-Rose Garden Plants
A. 'Joseph's Coat' (large-flowered climber) (1)
B. 'Peace' (hybrid tea) (3)
C. 'Olé' (grandiflora) (3)
D. 'Mister Lincoln' (hybrid tea) (3)
E. 'Oregold' (hybrid tea) (1)
F. 'Double Delight' (hybrid tea) (3)
G. 'Amber Queen' (floribunda) (3)
H. 'Showbiz' (floribunda) (4)
I. 'Class Act' (floribunda) (4)
J. 'Rainbow's End' (miniature) (12)
K. 'Beauty Secret' (miniature) (9)

Alternate Selections
A. 'Handel' (large-flowered climber) (1)
B. 'Lady X' (hybrid tea) (3)
C. 'White Lightnin'' (grandiflora) (3)
E. 'Pristine' (hybrid tea) (1)
F. 'Sonia' (grandiflora) (3)
G. 'Cherish' (floribunda) (3)
H. 'Europeana' (floribunda) (4)
I. 'Angel Face' (floribunda) (4)
J. 'Peaches 'n' Cream' (miniature) (12)
K. 'Toy Clown' (miniature) (9)

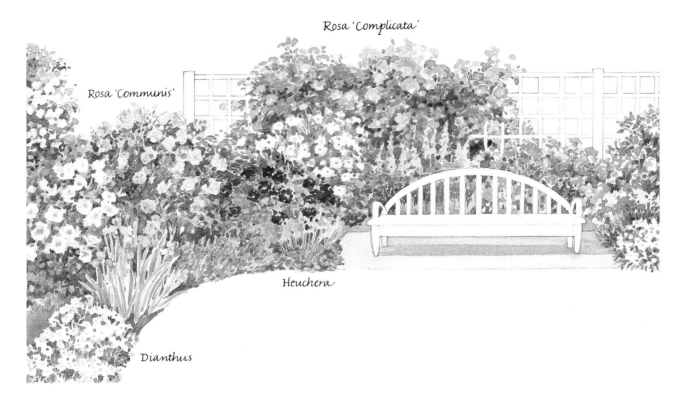

Rosa 'Complicata'

Rosa 'Communis'

Heuchera

Dianthus

A HERITAGE-ROSE GARDEN

In establishing a bed of heritage roses, you can transport yourself back in time to the gardens of the nineteenth century. A number of roses that were garden favorites in the 1800s have survived to the present day, cherished and preserved over the generations for their individual beauties and their link to a gracious time gone by. Some of these even were known to Napoleon's Empress Josephine, who maintained at Malmaison a renowned collection of all roses known to western Europe at that time.

Heritage-rose enthusiasts recognize two subdivisions among the great array of roses that developed before 1900. The old garden roses constitute the various classes that derive from European species and were in existence before 1800—the gallica, centifolia, damask, and alba roses. With few exceptions, all the old garden roses provide one lavish flowering in mid- to late spring. The introduction from the Orient of China roses, which flower repeatedly, brought about the development of various repeat-flowering classes—particularly the tea roses, China, Noisette, Bourbon, and hybrid

perpetuals—that culminated in the emergence of hybrid teas. The introduction in 1867 of the first hybrid tea, 'La France', can be thought of as the dawn of modern roses, though all roses developed before about 1910 (especially cultivars in the ninteenth-century classes) fall under the heritage umbrella.

This planting plan creates three different rose gardens. Roses in the main list are old garden roses. All give a sumptuous floral display in spring, then rest for the remainder of the year. This group has the broadest adaptability to climate, growing in zones 4 through 9 and needing no winter protection in the colder zones. In the first list of alternative selections, you'll find nineteenth-century roses that show their ancestry of the China roses: All flower repeatedly from spring through fall. Less cold tolerant than the old garden roses, these are best in zones 8, 9, and 10, although gardeners in zones 5, 6, and 7 may grow some of them—the Bourbon, hybrid perpetual, hybrid tea, Portland, and polyantha—if they protect the plants during the winter. The second list of alternatives offers twentieth-century shrub roses—technically not heritage roses, although

Heritage-Rose Garden Plants

A. 'Complicata' (gallica hybrid) (1)
B. 'Mme. Plantier' (alba hybrid) (1)
C. 'Communis' ('Common Moss') (centifolia moss) (1)
D. 'Alba Semi-plena' (*Rosa × alba* 'Semiplena') (alba) (1)
E. 'Marie Louise' (damask) (1)
F. 'Belle de Crecy' (gallica) (1)
G. 'Tuscany' (gallica) (1)
H. 'Mme. Hardy' (damask) (1)
I. 'Empress Josephine' (gallica hybrid) (1)
J. 'Rosa Mundi' (*R. gallica* 'Versicolor') (gallica) (1)
K. 'Celestial' (alba) (1)
L. 'Rose de Meaux' ('De Meaux') (centifolia) (1)
M. 'Burgundian Rose' ('Pompon de Bourgogne') (centifolia) (1)
N. *Iris* 'Pallida Variegata' (5)
O. *Nepeta × faassenii* (catmint) (7)
P. *Lavandula angustifolia* 'Munstead' (English lavender) (2)
Q. *Digitalis × mertonensis* (foxglove) (13)
R. *Coreopsis verticillata* 'Moonbeam' (coreopsis) (1)
S. *Dianthus plumarius* (cottage pink) (5)
T. *Achillea ×* 'Moonshine' (yarrow) (3)
U. *Aster × frikartii* (aster) (4)
V. *Teucrium chamaedrys* (germander) (3)
W. *Heuchera sanguinea* (coralbells) (4)

Alternative Selections I

A. 'Reve d'Or' (Noisette) (1)
B. 'Sombreuil' (climbing tea) (1)
C. 'Gruss an Teplitz' (Bourbon hybrid) (1)
D. 'Duchesse de Brabant' (tea) (1)
E. 'Archduke Charles' (China) (1)
F. 'Comte de Chambord' (Portland) (1)
G. 'La France' (hybrid tea) (1)
H. 'Cecile Brunner' (polyantha) (1)
I. 'Souv. de la Malmaison' (Bourbon) (1)
J. 'Reine des Violettes' (hybrid perpetual) (1)
K. 'Mme. Lambard' (tea) (1)
L. 'White Pet' ('Little White Pet') (polyantha) (1)
M. 'Old Blush' ('Parson's Pink China') (China) (1)

Alternative Selections II

A. 'Buff Beauty' (hybrid musk) (1)
B. 'Cornelia' (hybrid musk) (1)
C. 'Betty Prior' (floribunda) (1)
D. 'Iceberg' (floribunda) (1)
E. 'Bonica' (shrub) (1)
F. 'The Yeoman' (shrub) (1)
G. 'English Garden' (shrub) (1)
H. 'La Sevillana' (shrub) (1)
I. 'The Fairy' (polyantha) (1)
J. 'Carefree Beauty' (shrub) (1)
K. 'Nevada' (hybrid moyesii) (1)
L. 'Frau Dagmar Hartopp' (hybrid rugosa) (1)
M. 'Happy' (polyantha) (2)

individually and in mass they give a similar effect. Most are carried by heritage-rose growers. In cold tolerance, these fall between the roses in the first two lists. Most will need some winter protection in zones 4, 5, and 6; the exceptions are Carefree Beauty and Frau Dagmar Hartopp.

The roses on all three lists have the same cultural needs as modern roses: good soil, sun preferably for at least three quarters of the day, and regular watering. However, they are in general more forgiving of lapses in culture and turn in good performances with less cosseting than their modern relatives. They may fall prey to the same insects and diseases that bother modern roses, but their resistance is often varied; the teas, Noisettes, and some of the shrub roses are nearly immune to diseases.

Late winter or early spring, depending on climate, is the major maintenance time. First comes a general garden cleanup of dead leaves and spent stems from the perennials. Next, of course, is the rose pruning. These roses need less heading back than do modern roses. Use a light hand with the pruning shears, cutting out dead and weak wood, then pruning just to shape the plants. Prune the old garden roses in the main planting list as little as possible while they are dormant: Flowers come on growth produced the previous spring and summer. With these roses, save the job of removing old branches until just after flowering. Among the companion plants, late winter (in zones 8, 9, and 10) or early spring (in colder zones) also is the time to cut back the English lavender, germander, and (in zones 8, 9, and 10) the catmint by about half. During the growing and blooming period, watering and, perhaps, pest control constitute the maintenance agenda. As this planting matures over the years, most of the perennials will need dividing and replanting as they become crowded and their productivity diminishes.

Variations

The paved area with the bench separates this rose planting into two parts of similar shape but unequal size. For a smaller planting, you can eliminate all the roses and companion plants in the smaller portion to one side of the paved area, stopping the planting at the Empress Josephine or the Souv. de la Malmaison, or The Fairy.

Heritage-Rose Garden

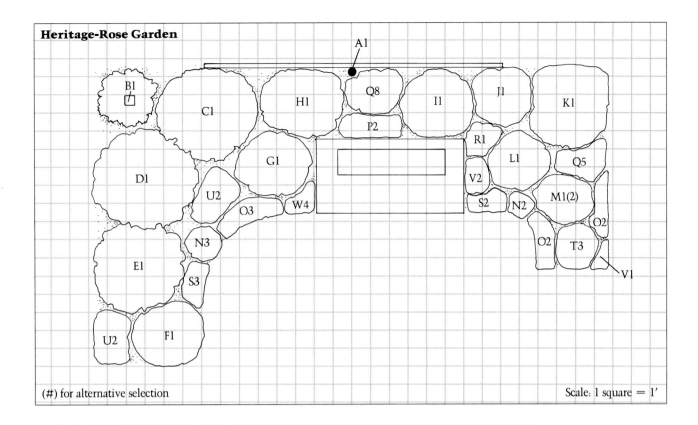

(#) for alternative selection   Scale: 1 square = 1′

Mail-Order Sources

I t is always most convenient to buy plants from local nurseries, where you can inspect your purchases and avoid the added cost of shipping. However, if you can't locate the plants you want locally, these mail-order sources offer a wide assortment of plants in the categories indicated.

Bluestone Perennials
7225 Middle Ridge Road
Madison, OH 44057
Perennials

Busse Gardens
Route 2, Box 238
Cokato, MN 55321
Perennials

Canyon Creek Nursery
3527 Dry Creek Road
Oroville, CA 95965
Perennials

Fieldstone Gardens, Inc.
620 Quaker Lane
Vassalboro, ME 04989
Perennials

Heritage Rose Gardens
16831 Mitchell Creek Drive
Fort Bragg, CA 95437
Heritage, shrub, and species roses

High Country Rosarium
1717 Downing at Park Avenue
Denver, CO 80218
Heritage, shrub, and species roses

Klehm Nursery
Route 5, Box 197
South Barrington, IL 60010
Perennials

Roses of Yesterday & Today
802 Brown's Valley Road
Watsonville, CA 95076
Heritage, shrub, and species roses

Thompson & Morgan, Inc.
Box 1308
Jackson, NJ 08527
Seeds: annuals, perennials, vegetables, shrubs

Andre Viette
Farm & Nursery, Route 1, Box 16
Fishersville, VA 11939
Perennials

Wayside Gardens
1 Garden Lane
Hodges, SC 29695
Perennials, vines, shrubs, heritage roses, trees

White Flower Farm
Litchfield, CT 06759
Perennials, vines, shrubs

Climate Zone Map

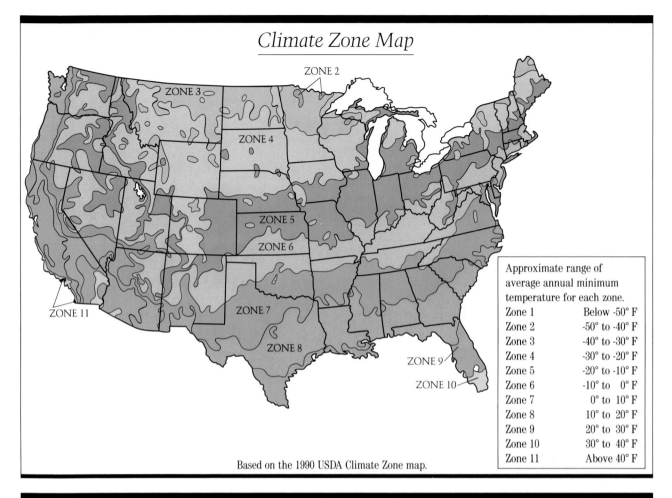

ZONE 2
ZONE 3
ZONE 4
ZONE 5
ZONE 6
ZONE 7
ZONE 8
ZONE 9
ZONE 10
ZONE 11

Approximate range of average annual minimum temperature for each zone.

Zone 1	Below -50° F
Zone 2	-50° to -40° F
Zone 3	-40° to -30° F
Zone 4	-30° to -20° F
Zone 5	-20° to -10° F
Zone 6	-10° 0° F
Zone 7	0° to 10° F
Zone 8	10° to 20° F
Zone 9	20° to 30° F
Zone 10	30° to 40° F
Zone 11	Above 40° F

Based on the 1990 USDA Climate Zone map.

U.S. Measure and Metric Measure Conversion Chart

		Formulas for Exact Measures			Rounded Measures for Quick Reference		
	Symbol	When you know:	Multiply by:	To find:			
Mass (Weight)	oz	ounces	28.35	grams	1 oz		= 30 g
	lb	pounds	0.45	kilograms	4 oz		= 115 g
	g	grams	0.035	ounces	8 oz		= 225 g
	kg	kilograms	2.2	pounds	16 oz	= 1 lb	= 450 g
					32 oz	= 2 lb	= 900 g
					36 oz	= 2¼ lb	= 1000g (1 kg)
Volume	pt	pints	0.47	liters	1 c	= 8 oz	= 250 ml
	qt	quarts	0.95	liters	2 c (1 pt)	= 16 oz	= 500 ml
	gal	gallons	3.785	liters	4 c (1 qt)	= 32 oz	= 1 liter
	ml	milliliters	0.034	fluid ounces	4 qt (1 gal)	= 128 oz	= 3¾ liter
Length	in.	inches	2.54	centimeters	⅜ in.	= 1 cm	
	ft	feet	30.48	centimeters	1 in.	= 2.5 cm	
	yd	yards	0.9144	meters	2 in.	= 5 cm	
	mi	miles	1.609	kilometers	2½ in.	= 6.5 cm	
	km	kilometers	0.621	miles	12 in. (1 ft)	= 30 cm	
	m	meters	1.094	yards	1 yd	= 90 cm	
	cm	centimeters	0.39	inches	100 ft	= 30 m	
					1 mi	= 1.6 km	
Temperature	°F	Fahrenheit	⅝ (after subtracting 32)	Celsius	32°F	= 0°C	
	°C	Celsius	⅝ (then add 32)	Fahrenheit	212°F	= 100°C	
Area	in.²	square inches	6.452	square centimeters	1 in.²	= 6.5 cm²	
	ft²	square feet	929.0	square centimeters	1 ft²	= 930 cm²	
	yd²	square yards	8361.0	square centimeters	1 yd²	= 8360 cm²	
	a.	acres	0.4047	hectares	1 a.	= 4050 m²	